My Big Dead Rabbit

By Suzanne DiTommaso

JOHN 8:36

BE FREE INDEED!

Copyright 2012
All rights reserved.
Suzanne M. DiTommaso

To those who carried *me*,
Thank you.

Prologue
The rabbit dream. February 2011

His fur dark and light grey and was so soft. I think it was a boy. I never looked. He was huge. Like a big, oversized stuffed animal only he was a real rabbit upside down in my arms. His body was soft and squishy. I didn't know what his face looked like; I could only see his soft tummy and his floppy, furry legs. He was belly up in my arms and he had a big zipper down his middle. I could unzip and zip him and his insides looked exactly as my mind imagines real rabbit innards would look like. He wasn't bloody at all, just guts and entrails when I opened him. The fur around his zipper was starting to get caught and the flesh around the zipper was starting to become fairly mangled. I held him as I rode the bus. I loved him. I needed him. I didn't want him to die.

Several people gave me odd looks. I didn't know anyone on the bus, and yet they were not strangers to me.

"That rabbit is dead." One woman said. I dismissed her comment and stared out the window.

"Honey, I think he's a lost cause." Another woman whispered in my ear. Again, I looked away. One by one throughout the journey people would tell me my rabbit was dead. There were times in the journey when no one was looking and I would unzip the zipper and look around inside to see if there were any signs of life. Then, fearing I would be discovered, I would zip him back up, arrange his fur and hold my

sleeping rabbit. Again and again this happened and I began to fear that he might actually be dead.

It was a very long journey and I have no idea how much time had passed. I was standing at this point with my rabbit in my arms and a man was trying to get past me. He, like the others, looked at me with pity and gently told me what I didn't want to hear.

"Honey, if he really is alive, he's probably better off free, don't you think?" he asked.

I didn't like what I heard but I looked at my sleeping rabbit and made the difficult decision to set him free. I remember opening the window and hugging him close. My heart was breaking to let him go but if he was really alive, he should be free. It didn't make sense to set him free because in my heart I knew the truth. But it didn't make sense to keep holding him either. He was heavy and not easy to get out the window but I was able to heave him out. He landed with a thud; a big thud and his big limp body flopped unnaturally on his neck. He was obviously dead, and very dead. He was my big, dead rabbit.

I felt mixed about not having him, a sort of sad freedom. I looked away quickly and tried not to think about his absence. Suddenly I looked back but he was gone.

Chapter One

Boston's "More Than a Feeling" flowed from the 8-track and clicked over as I turned onto Oakland Avenue. I popped my VW out of second gear and coasted down the street in hopes of finding a parking space. I had become quite proficient at parallel parking in my short few months of attending a new school in Pittsburgh. I had no need for parallel parking in Mars, PA, where I had grown up in a very rural farmhouse but I was different and more sophisticated now. My mum taught me to drive a stick shift up the very long driveway on the farm. In fact, I can remember steering up the driveway on her lap ever since I was able to draw out the word *please* enough to convince her to give in.

Ah, a spot. I expertly maneuvered my little Volkswagen Dasher into the space and hoped there wasn't street cleaning the next day because I planned to be there overnight. I crushed out my Marlboro Light in the ashtray and sighed at the ever growing pile of McDonalds bags on my floor. Cranking up the driver's side window I noticed the red and white checkered curtain of the fourth floor move. *Oh good, she saw me*, I thought. I gave the parking brake a good tug and made sure the car was in gear. I reached behind me awkwardly and blindly located my duffle bag. It was heavy and I had to struggle it through the two front seats. I climbed out and smelled the smells of the city in the spring. It was late May and I had just finished my junior year of high school at my new school. It was warm and the sun was still high in the sky at 6 p.m. Duffle bag in hand I locked my car with the key and trotted across the street to the big sandstone building and up the three front steps and past the numbers 407. I hadn't even entered the first set of doors when I heard the piercing sound of the door buzzer. Quickly I lurched for the second door and just snagged it before the buzzer stopped. *Gosh, give me a sec*, I thought.

Once inside, I started my way up the wide, wrapping stairwell. The whole building smelled of stale cigarettes and old brick. The stairwell was eerily quiet; it always was. I never saw one single person in that hallway. They were all mysterious characters with secret lives behind closed doors with muffled televisions humming. I was breathless as I reached the fourth floor and entered the first set of doors. This led to a long, windowless corridor and Suzette's apartment door was at the very end waiting for me in the dark. I reached up to knock but I heard the deadbolt turn.

"Hey mama," She said coolly as she opened the door. She called everyone "Mama".

"Hey." I said

"Everyone's on their way, I'm just headed for the shower," she said as if I couldn't tell by her towel wrapped appearance.

"Ok...I'm allowed to stay the night," I announced as I made my way into the living room.

"Ok Baby," she said as if she didn't care one way or another. You were Baby, Mama or Mommy to Suzette. She disappeared into the bathroom and left the door wide open.

I heard the shower start and I settled in on the couch and popped a can of Diet Coke that I had pulled out of my bag. I raked around in my purse and found my box of Marlboro Lights which I set on the coffee table next to hers. I opened her box and took out her lighter.

"So, who's coming?" I shouted down the hall to the open bathroom door. I could hear her humming something I didn't recognize. I gave up and sat back on the couch. The room was old and full of old, eclectic furniture with bright colored tapestries adorning the walls. I felt a gentle nudge to look down and see Bacardi, Suzette's cat nuzzling my leg and purring from the Oriental rug.

"Hey you," I whispered and pulled Bacardi up on my lap.

I cuddled with Bacardi until the shower eventually stopped and Suzette waltzed through the living room in a small towel. She was small and very pretty. She wasn't the standard of beauty I had been accustomed to up until this time in my life. We were very different. She was light skinned and black, with big dark eyes and lots of black curly hair. She was thin and small in stature but very outspoken. I was blonde, pale, full of round curves and very shy. I had worn a pink shaker knit sweater backwards and white Capri pants with a long string of pearls. I felt pretty in it and my hair was perfectly permed.

"Shannon and Jason will be here…and Donna of course…and some of my friends from the academy…and maybe even…the Cavemen," she said, popping her head in the doorway with a big grin.

"Cavemen?" I asked following her into the kitchen.

"They're just some guys. You know the kind of guys who drag you around by your hair," she said putting a pint of Bacardi rum on the table, breaking the seal and unscrewing the cap.

"Oh…yeah," I said, thoroughly confused but a little intrigued.

"You'll see Mommy," she said and disappeared into her room with her glass of rum and Coke.

"Help yourself," she shouted and I looked at the rum. I didn't have any interest in alcohol and thought I would like to drink the Coke because it was not diet but I had to think of my figure.

"Nah," I said going back into the living room and plopping on the couch.

The unmistakable buzzer sounded again.

"That's probably Donna," she said as she appeared in nothing but a bra and panties to hit the buzzer button.

"I could have done that," I said. She smiled and exaggeratedly wiggled back to her room.

I heard footsteps down the corridor and opened the door for Donna to enter the apartment, now quite full of light blue smoke.

"What's up?" she said to me. "Hi Suz!" she shouted to the back of the apartment.

"The *Cavemen* are coming…maybe," I said

She looked at me and smiled. I felt pointedly sixteen and very naïve.

The guests began to arrive for our party and I relaxed and just took it all in. It was all new but I was having fun and these people were so sophisticated and very far from anything I knew. The food on the coffee table was very meager just chips, pretzels and whatever we could scrounge from leftover fries and wings in the fridge. It wasn't like the parties my parents had when the people brought dishes of lovely appetizers to show off their culinary skills. Most of us came empty handed. Just cigarettes I think, and that was a great contribution.

The party turned to a blur and people milled around and lounged coolly on the old furniture trying to look as sarcastic and ironic as possible.

The Cure was playing loudly when at about 11 p.m. a group of men arrived. *These must be the cavemen,* I thought. They arrived in a pack and they were loud, insulting and boisterous. There were 5 or 6 of them. One of them spoke in a strong Spanish or Puerto Rican accent (I didn't know the difference.) I was perched on the green velvet chair which I believe was a dumpster treasure when Suzette slid right in next to me.

"Steve asked me what's up with you," she said and I looked over toward the group.

"What's up with me?"

"Don't look!" she said and made her eyes very big.

"Sorry," I whispered.

"What do you think?" she asked without moving her head.

"Which one is he?" I said without moving my head or my lips.

"White tank." her mouth was contorted sideways.

"Oh…he's cute I guess." I said. I didn't know what I was supposed to be thinking really. I couldn't really see him but from what I could make out he was a big guy with dark hair and glasses.

"Ok." She said and scurried off Bacardi and Coke in hand.

Next I remember Steve was boldly sitting with me in the chair. We were pushed together and I was very uncomfortable but tried to act aloof. He was very obvious in his attraction and I found it quite intoxicating. He didn't reveal anything about himself. He was gentle and nicer than he looked and certainly nicer than I would expect from a *caveman*.

We sat up all night talking and when the sun came up he said he wanted to see me again. I was game and gave him my number. I had no idea how old he was or if my parents would approve but now that I was 16 and had a car and some freedom I realized they didn't need to know anything about him. I had no idea how much that meeting would alter the course of my life forever.

I was becoming quite familiar with the Pittsburgh area and Steve and I became quite serious quite quickly. He worked at the local beer distributor and I frequently picked him up after work.

One particular evening I pulled up in front of the beer distributor and turned off my car. He was not on his stool out front. I was confused but I waited and waited. Eventually someone else came out and took his stool in, shut the door and turned off the lights. I was even more confused. He told me he was working that night and I should pick him up at the normal time. I drove up and down the surrounding streets looking for him but he was nowhere to be found. I decided to go up to overlook at the park and see if he was there.

I pulled into the circle and a group was gathered there in the dark. I could see the intermittent amber glow of cigarettes and occasionally I heard a familiar voice so I approached the group cautiously.

"You guys seen Steve?" I called out as I approached. A dark figure came toward me. It was one of Steve's friends.

"Glenn's dead." Beanie said emerging from the crowd. I stood in shocked silence. Glenn was Steve's best friend. We had just seen him the night before.

"What…dead?"

"He was on his motorcycle and hit a telephone pole." I couldn't think straight. I had very little experience with death.

"Oh my God." I said.

"Steve's gone. We don't know where he went. He's pretty messed up."

"Ok. Oh my God." I said rushing to my car.

I got in my car and drove through the dark streets of the park. I went to all the little coves, hollows and usual places until eventually I saw him. He was sitting on a stone wall all alone at the side of the road at the bottom of the hill. I walked up to him and his face was wet with tears. He stared emotionless into the night. He had been drinking which he didn't do much and the alcohol smell was strong.

"Glenn's dead." He said without any emotion.

"I know." I whispered trying to hug him.

He pushed me away and jumped down off the wall. He started to leave but eventually turned and buried his face in my shoulder. He was broken-hearted and I could feel his body trembling.

"Take me there." He mumbled.

"Where?"

"To the last spot where he was alive." He said his voice muffled into my shoulder.

"I know where it is." He said and took my hand.

We got into my VW and drove in silence. He did know exactly where Glenn had died but I didn't know where we were. We stopped on the side of the road, got out and walked up to the pole. I stared at the big gash in the wood where there had been an impact. There were flowers already on the ground and there was a patch of oil with some sawdust. I continued to stare at the gash in the pole. It was unbelievable that Glenn was there one instant and gone the next, right at that spot. I had not had much experience with sudden death, or death at all really.

Steve sat on the ground by the pole with his head in his hands. This was bigger than I felt capable of handling. He was experiencing memories I didn't have, a friendship I had barely seen, I felt very alone almost like I was in the wrong place and this was a big mistake. *I hardly know him.* I thought.

"I need to go to his house," he said without looking at me.

"Ok." I had no idea what that would be like or even where that was.

We sat in silence as we made our way to Glenn's house. Upstairs around the kitchen table there were adults.

"Stevie!" cried a woman with very tired, swollen eyes and she jumped into Steve's arms.

I wondered if that was Glenn's mother. She began to wail and scream as they held each other. She started to fall to the ground and Steve and another man gently got her into a chair in the other room. Steve made his way around the table and hugged and cried with all of them. One man got up and went out a screen door which closed with a bang. He worked his way through the house and hugged and held most of the people in the upstairs as I stood in the shadows.

There were so many people there. Eventually we went to the basement where the kids were. There were beer bottles everywhere and the blue smoke was thick. The people were barely visible through the smoke sitting with their arms around each other on low profile couches. I didn't know any of them.

I felt like an outsider that day with the kids and the parents. In fact, we didn't see much of anyone's parents in that group. Steve did not know his father; at least I don't think he did. His father was definitely not in the picture. I'd heard that Steve had been in a fight and someone had almost died at his hand. I think he had been in a juvenile detention center. I was so young and naïve and I think in my heart of hearts, I just didn't believe any of that was true. He never really talked about it. In fact, he said he didn't want to talk about it *ever*. So, I was happy in my ignorance and on his arm. I was really sad for him. My life was so ideal in comparison. My parents weren't even divorced.

Most of my friends had to at least deal with that. I had my own car and a private school education, pocket money, a curfew, the works. I saw two sides of life in my new adventure in Pittsburgh, the extremely well off and the other end of the spectrum.

We left Glenn's house and drove back through the park. I had never seen Steve cry before. Even though we had known each other just a few short weeks and we didn't really know each other, I did feel very close to him. He had become very important to me.

Emotions were very raw in the air that night. Life and death was all around us. I was so aware of my own heartbeat. It seemed so big, the living and the dead separated by only one tiny second.

In that moment staring at him with tears in his eyes and his broken heart, I could feel nothing but my heart beating for him. I felt it was unfair and too big for us to deal with, death. How could Glenn be dead? What was it? Dead. The word itself was so final. We would never ever see him again. He would never change and even his hair would never grow again. His parents would never see him again, ever. He would not grow up, he would not get married. It was over. Forever over and no one could change that. Steve had lost his best friend for the rest of his life and we were all teetering on this tiny wire of life and death.

We drove back to his house and went into his room. Lying on the mattress on the floor in the dark I wasn't sure if I was alive or dead. Were any of us promised anything? Will any of us make it through life?

He was suddenly very still and his voice was flat. He sounded scary and robotic. I was afraid he had turned off all his emotions. What if he couldn't love again? I wanted to comfort him and make him feel loved and sure of us the way I did. So I gave him what I thought would make him feel loved. Me.

I regretted it instantly and I think he did too. We were so young. I found myself in his little dark bathroom staring out into the dark with the sound of the traffic buzzing by and the whir of the washing machine in the next room. Slowly I came back into his room and stood in the dark.

"You okay?" he was standing now.

"Um yeah."

"Come back." he said putting his arms around me but I couldn't feel anything.

"You're on the pill right?"

"Oh – right," I said. *Dear God, what had I done?*

Chapter Two

It was late afternoon and the sun was warm on my face as I lay on my blanket on the ground with the long grass all around me. There was a gentle breeze and I could smell the hayfields that were still green.

The very top of Old Orchard Hill overlooked an apple orchard and the trees below were bursting with fruit. The hillcrest was the highest point in the entire valley and our house way below was like a spec and was the only visible house for miles. Lying in the grass nothing was in view but sky. I sat up and inched myself sideways toward the big gray rabbit. I took a long pause drinking him in.

"So, are you real?" I asked. The rabbit looked up at me.

"What do you think?" he said looking away and lifting his head to the breeze.

"I guess what I mean is, are you dead?"

"Do you want me to be?"

"No, of course not."

"Are you sure?"

I had to think about that one. Finally I said, "No, I don't want you to be dead."

"Hmmm," his rabbit nose quivered. I looked at his rabbit eyes, and they seemed to be very wise.

"We don't have long," he said. "I'm going to be leaving, really leaving. One day soon you'll be able to let me go, and you'll be okay without me, just

like you were before. You were okay before I came, weren't you?"

"Oh yes," I said, "I was just fine before you came." I remembered fondly. "But," I paused. "I can't live without you. Plus, there's no one else to take care of you." I reached over and pulled up a handful of grass and held it out to him.

"Yes you can and yes there is." He took a couple of strands of grass. Chewing he searched my face. He cocked his head to the side.

"Tell me about it," he said. "Tell me how it was before I came."

It was later that summer and Glenn's death had faded into the background in my mind. I was lying on a raft in my friend Julie's pool back in the suburbs away from the city and the city world I now knew existed. Steve and I were still seeing each other but had sort of cooled off a little. I think we both knew we were moving way too fast. Julie and I loved our summers together. It was midweek and life was very lazy for the two of us. We just worked on our tans and planned where we would drive around that night.

Her family had an above ground pool which by today's standards isn't much but to us it was Disney Land. Her Dad was teasing us as he always did, and we were having a wonderful time. Julie's house was like a second home to me. Her parents were liberal and loving and they treated us like adults. I spent many hours at that house and we did a lot of laughing.

I was feeling the sun on my face and enjoying the sounds of summer and smells of suntan lotion when an unwelcome thought abruptly popped into my head. Where was my period? I did some quick calculations. *Something isn't right.* Slowly the thought process became more intense. *Wait, I must have missed something, or maybe I had one that I didn't remember?* I began counting and adding and straining to remember. I tried to block it out but I couldn't help the thought creeping into my brain. *The night that Glenn died?* No, that couldn't be. Something else was wrong. It wasn't that.

Later that evening we were doing our usual preparations in Julie's bedroom for a night out. She was at her lighted mirror finishing her make up while her mother made us pizza. The smell was wafting down the hall and it was so comforting. I could hear the crickets outside. I so loved summer. I was ready for our night out but my mind was distracted, very distracted. I stood staring at her and I couldn't seem to keep my stomach from flip-flopping.

"Julie," I said gently closing the door.

"Huh?" she said while puckering and applying her signature red lipstick.

"I'm late."

"For what?" She wasn't looking at me.

Suddenly her head snapped from her own reflection. "Late late?' she said as she dropped her head forward as if she was looking over glasses.

"Yes, late late."

"Sh..." her voice trailed off. "Are you sure? How late?" She spun her whole body toward me.

"I don't know," I said and I felt a big lump in my throat. Just then I felt something pushing against the door.

"You girls ok? Why is your door closed?" Her mother pushed the door and came into the room. She looked back and forth at us.

"Pizza's ready." she said with suspicious eyes.

She looked at Julie and then at me.

"Suz, you ok?"

"Yes, yes, my allergies are so bad in the spring. I get allergy shots. I probably need one."

"Oh, ok," she said lovingly. "Well, come and eat before it gets cold."

We went out to the kitchen and I tried to eat. I couldn't taste anything and I felt sick to my stomach.

"You really don't look good Suzie. Maybe you girls should stay in," her mother said looking very directly at Julie. Julie's eyes searched mine and I nodded.

"Yeah, you're probably right. We'll just hang out in my room tonight, right Suz?'

~ 22 ~

"Yeah, okay," I said trying to make my throat work as I swallowed a small bit of cheese.

"Thanks for the pizza. I'm just not myself tonight," I said as I excused myself from the table. I stood in their small bathroom fearing I might be sick when Julie poked her head around the door.

"Come on Suz. I'm sure you're fine. Come into my room."

Julie raked around her purse and pulled out her little Hallmark calendar.

"When was your last period?" She asked flipping the pages and finding June in her book.

"I can't remember. I just can't remember," I said over and over. It was now July and June seemed ages ago. We tried to recreate some events we could remember.

"It wasn't Kelly's graduation party weekend, right?"

"No," I said with great certainty.

"What about that weekend when we were at Sam's cabin?"

"No," I said and I was beginning to understand just how long it had been.

"I never had a period in June," I finally admitted.

"Sure you did," she said trying to comfort me. "You just don't remember."

We stayed up in her room and she tried to make me feel better, but I was terrified when I laid my head on the pillow that night. I tried to put the fear out of my head and I tried to continue on with my life.

Days and nights came and went and still nothing. My 17th birthday arrived and I had plans to go into the city. I had gone shopping that day and came home. I drove up the long driveway to our farmhouse and I was wearing white overalls. My dad was doing something in front of the barn in the driveway. He looked concerned and walked over to my window.

"Suzie, there's oil all over your car," he said, verging on anger.

"There is?" I said naively.

He asked me to pop the hood. There was oil everywhere. He then got quite angry with me.

"Oh Suz! Obviously you didn't replace the oil cap when you added oil." He was really mad. "You're all in white, stand back so you don't ruin your white clothes!"

The pregnancy fear popped into my head for a split second and I stood way back so I could stay pure and white in front of my dad. I watched him clean up all the oil and he found the oil cap in the engine somewhere. As he worked his anger subsided.

"You're lucky the cap was still in there. Ok, you're all set. Don't do that again, okay

Suz?" he said and he gave me a little hug and blessed me with a kiss as I went off into the city for my birthday night out.

Weeks passed and I tried not to allow any thought or belief into my head that it could be true.

Eventually however, I came to the distressing realization that I would need to go to a clinic and have a test just so I could sleep at night. I told Julie and we sat in her room and looked in a phone book. The clinic was very far away and it was a long drive. I had no clue where to get a pregnancy test and I think Julie and I just called the first number in the book.

I waited in the lobby just wanting that relief so I could go on with my life. I was certain they would say I was not pregnant, that something else was wrong and I should see my doctor. A nurse walked into the room, looked me square in the eye.

"Your test is positive," she said point-blank.

I couldn't hear or feel anything after that. It was like I imagined being on a sinking ship, red lights and sirens everywhere. The regular power systems have failed, panic is everywhere, it's dark and all you can hear are sirens and the water coming in. How can you think with all that noise and commotion? How can you think about anything other than a way out?

We drove back to Julie's house and said very little. She never asked me what I was going to do. I don't think I thought about it. I couldn't think of anything. My brain was shutting down from all the panic. We got back to Julie's house and I walked into her room and closed the door. Anxiously I dialed the phone. He wasn't home.

"Hi um, this is Suzie. Could you please have Steve call me? I'm at Julie's."

He knew I was late. He knew I was going for a test. Where was he?

Eventually the phone rang and Julie and I stared at each other. I answered the phone and the first words on the other end of the line stayed with me to this day.

"So the rabbit died huh?" Those are the only words I remember him saying. The words seemed to be spinning around me. *Rabbit? What rabbit? Dead rabbit? What was he talking about?* I stood speechless, what did that mean?

"Um, yeah I guess so," I said with no idea what I was claiming.

Chapter Three

The rabbit hopped up onto my leg and wobbled a bit before resting his head against me. I put my arms around him. He felt so familiar. He was big and gray. He was very many colors of gray all blending together. I stroked him behind his ears and down his back. He was soft, very soft.

"Once upon a time," he said, "there was a thing called the rabbit test. Do you know about that?"

"Someone said it to me once," I told him. "Someone said the rabbit died."

"A lot of us died," the rabbit said. "In fact we all died. That was a long time ago. It's all different these days. It used to be a big deal to find out if you were pregnant, and if you really, really wanted to know, well, you took a rabbit test and waited for the results. They injected rabbits, and then they opened us up and looked at our ovaries."

"That sounds horrible, like they unzipped you and looked inside," I said stroking his ears.

"Just the females of course… I personally don't have any ovaries. You know that, don't you, because you keep looking inside me."

"I'm sorry for doing that. I don't know what ovaries look like though. So, you're a boy?"

"Rabbits don't normally have zippers," my rabbit reminded me and ignoring my question continued. "So when they opened them up, the rabbits died. That's the rabbit test. It was a big deal."

"Yuck, yeah I guess so."

    I drove home alone in silence, no radio, just me and my dread. I knew I should go home but first I drove around for a while thinking and avoiding thinking. How was I going to do this? How was I going to tell my parents? I knew deep down that I needed my mother. What would she say? There was no way she could fix it. I had gotten myself in a situation that my mother could not fix even if she wanted to.

    I went to Hardee's and sat in the drive through. I didn't know what I should eat or if I even could eat. I left with nothing. Maybe I could just disappear? Maybe I could just run away? Maybe I could get myself into a car accident and I wouldn't be pregnant after the trauma. That would work, or maybe if I died…?

    After some time I resigned to the fact that I had nowhere else to go but home. I loved our home and that was the best place I could be right then. Eventually I made my way up the driveway to our big, old farmhouse.

    I sat in the driveway staring at my home. It was blue when we moved in but now it was green, although I don't remember it being painted. It was light green with dark green shutters. It was in the middle of a big valley, our valley. I had lived there since I was five. I knew every inch of those many acres. My brother and

I knew every curve and flow of the creek that ran through the pasture. I buried my first official pet, Chester the Mouse up on the hill in a clearing in the pine trees. We had, at various times, chickens and sheep, horses and ponies, gardens and crop fields. I would spend hours off in the woods on my own, on horseback or on foot. I was content and I don't think I ever felt lonely.

Occasionally, I would encounter Domino, our big black cat as she was hunting or Elsie would dash across the path up ahead and frighten the wits out of me. I would leave the house in the morning during the summer and come back when it got dark and throughout the day I encountered many creatures and no humans. Life was so simple.

We also had a Springer Spaniel named Holly. She was truly a great dog. She was brown and white and had a perpetual grin on her face. She would go for hours on long hikes and come home after great battles with groundhogs and she would dig hole after hole. She was always completely filthy, with great clumps of mud hanging from her curly once white legs. She even had mud in her mouth most times.

Holly had a soft mouth and one summer she raided every bunny nest in the valley and brought them home to us as a gift. One after another, day after day she placed them on the big, spindle front porch. My parents put them in a big glass tank with a heating lamp but most of them died.

One afternoon while wandering on the farm I noticed a sleeping baby bunny near the front path. It was wet and tiny and its eyes were closed. I reached down to pick it up and cradled it in my hand. Its guts squished out the side onto my hand like spaghetti and I dropped it quickly and gasped.   It hadn't looked dead lying in the grass but it certainly was very dead.

Holly was a very sweet but very odd dog. She also used to "pay" to come into the house with a stone. One, single stone from the driveway would be placed on the doorstep when she wanted to come in the house. Perhaps that's what the bunnies were about. Holly also had an amazing gag reflex. We were all so used to it and paid absolutely no attention when she would begin just softly gagging. It would gently grow into a retch and soon the retching volume and repetition would increase and it became stronger and stronger until she finally made a horrendous vomiting noise, but nothing, absolutely nothing came out. It never did. Not a hair ball, not spit, not a groundhog specimen, nothing. We didn't mind it actually. We accepted her just the way she was.

My parents had fantastic parties there. I specifically remember one party was a Shakespearian theme and everyone came in Mid

Summer Night's Dream costumes. We drank from silver goblets, there was an actual choir and I got to dress as a princess. My dress was white and I had a pointy hat with a scarf poking out the top. I have wonderful memories of that farm.

    I sat in the car and savored the last few minutes of my innocent youth. I looked up at the big farmhouse with the big spindle porch. The trees had all their leaves, the flowers were all in bloom and it was that time of year when it looked like a postcard. Years of memories flooded my heart. I pictured myself as a little girl sitting on a blanket on the lawn eating grapes with my Mum and playing "Run Down" with my dad and brother in the evenings. I looked to the pasture and longed to see Choctaw, my old appaloosa, and climb up on him and ride off over Old Orchard Hill. I longed to be anywhere but where I was. Anywhere but in this "condition" I was in.

    Eventually, I walked slowly up the path, took a deep breath of the smell of the summer lilacs and sycamore trees and went into the house the screen door slamming behind me.

I was unable to approach my parents all day. I thought about not telling them. But, what was I going to do? I was trapped in my own head. I was trapped in my own pregnant body. I was physically sick all day. We finished watching TV together and I said good night.

I went to my room. I reached under my pillow and put on my long green nightgown. It was bright green with yellow piping and a slit up each side of the legs. I had had it for as long as I could remember. I stood in my bedroom for a long time anticipating the horror which was about to unfold, aching in my stomach because I was about to break my mother's heart. Fearing she would tell my dad and he would be ashamed of me.

I walked to the top of the stairs and opened my mouth to call for her but nothing came out. Again I tried and again I was unable to make any sound. I sat on the landing step and took a big breath. I tried again and this time her name came out. I cringed. She didn't come right away. I called again. This time she appeared at the bottom of the stairs and her face was full of concern. As she was ascending the stairs I walked into her bedroom and sat on the bed. She entered the room cautiously and stared at me. Gently and silently she sat down next to me.

"What is it dear?" she said as she stroked my hair. I turned and looked at her and her face went white.

"Are you in some kind of trouble?" she stammered. I nodded. Her hand dropped. She sat in silence for a long time.

"Are you...are you pregnant?" She asked eventually as if she didn't want to ask. Again, I nodded. She gasped and stood up. She walked out of the room and I heard the panic in her voice as she called down the stairs, "Graham!"

My dad came up the stairs and I couldn't hear or see much. The room was spinning and I wanted the ground to swallow me up.

"She's pregnant," I heard my Mum say quietly. She sounded very angry.

There was some muffled dialogue as I sat and stared at the blue carpeted floor.

"Do you know what you are going to do?" one of them asked.

I remember Steve asked me that question too. I heard my dad go downstairs and my mother told me he was calling our minister, Father Eaton. I remember thinking that was futile. Yes, I knew what I was going to do.

"I'm getting rid of it!" I blurted to my Mum.

I wasn't sure when that thought had cemented itself in my heart but it was there and it was serious. There was nothing anyone could say to stop me. My dad appeared in the doorway and I was told I had an appointment to meet with Father Eaton the next day. I went to bed and cried.

I was lying in the dark on my wet pillow when I heard the door open. My dad quietly came into my room and sat on my bed in the dark. I was lying on my side facing away from him on my pillow.

He told me that he and my Mum had been up talking and they wanted me to know that if I had the baby I would not be alone. They would support me and we would make it work. I didn't move.

"Suzie, we don't want you to…," he said and put his hand on my back.

I squeezed my eyes shut and pretended to be asleep. He sat on my bed for what felt like an eternity and eventually he got up and I heard the door gently close.

Chapter 4

"Actually, I don't think you are real." I said suddenly feeling defensive. "I think you are just a figment of my imagination."

"Really?" the rabbit looked hurt.

"Yes, really," I insisted but I knew I was probably wrong and then feeling guilty I said, "Look, the thing is it's complicated. I don't even know how to take care of a rabbit. You don't want to stay here with me, right? I mean, you want to be free, don't you?" He was sitting very close to me and I wanted so much to hug him but I leaned away.

"Why do you keep holding me then? You're the one who keeps me." His little nose twitched and he was leaning on my leg. He looked out onto the field again as if he wanted to go.

"Run away then!" I said emphatically. "Just go!" I put my hand on his tail and gently pushed him. He was heavier than he looked so I pushed harder.

"You're mean," he said and looked back at me.

"I'm not mean but you shouldn't be here." I started to raise my voice. "You just shouldn't be here!" He jumped forward one time and looked back.

"If I did run away, what would you do? I can run pretty fast I am, after all, a rabbit."

"Oh….I don't know." I moved forward picking him up. I pulled him up to my face. "I don't know what to do. I'm sorry. I'm not mean," I sobbed.

"Please don't say I'm mean. Can't you just go, on your own, just go?"

"Nope," he said dropping his head. "You have to make me go."

I don't remember making the decision to have an abortion. It wasn't a decision I made. In fact, nobody made that choice. Nobody suggested it. It seemed to be the plan from the first minute. The moment when Steve had said "So the rabbit died?" seemed to be a defining moment. I didn't know what rabbit he was talking about but he didn't say he would take care of me. He didn't say we would get through this together. He didn't say anything at all.

I had twice been asked, "Do you know what *you* are going to do?" I realized quickly that I needed to make a plan to solve this problem without much discussion. It was the only way to escape that sinking ship. I don't remembering thinking about it at all. My only thought was finding the money and finding a clinic.

I think Steve's friend knew of a place. I was told at some point that if you are up to 12 weeks along its $250, if you are 12-15 weeks it's $500 and the price goes up from there. Well, that was certainly incentive enough to make a young, scared girl make a choice and quickly. I have no recollection of where it was or where we got the money, but I knew I was in a desperate hurry. Someone made an appointment; it wasn't me.

I met Father Eaton in an elementary school classroom because we had no church building at that time. He was already there waiting for me and when I walked in he stood up and half smiled. He was not very happy with me but he was loving and gentle. I sat in a small chair awkwardly.

"Tell me what's going on," he said warmly.

"I'm not having a baby, that's what's going on," I said defiantly.

"I understand that's what you want to do. I have to tell you Suzie, that it's not ok in God's eyes to terminate your pregnancy. I have to tell you that I don't know what the repercussions would be…only God knows."

"Are you talking about hell?" I asked.

"It's not for me to say, Suzie," he said sympathetically.

I heard him but his words were meaningless I did not have time to waiver or to consider what he might be saying. The clock was ticking and I was getting more and more pregnant with every second that ticked. I did not respond.

I stood up and walked out. My silence was quite painful I'm sure and I never went back to his church again.

At some point the next day my Dad had requested Steve come to the house. I went to the city to get him and brought him out to the farm. My dad's eyes were sad when he walked up. I was not permitted to hear the conversation. He and my dad stayed outside on the big spindle porch. I waited in the kitchen with my Mum in virtual silence until they were done.

Finally I heard the front door open. Steve walked in looking pale and shell shocked and nodded his readiness to leave. My dad did not come in. I don't know where he went. We drove back into the city and Steve never said a word about it. I don't know if I asked or not. I dropped him off at his house and drove back to the farm.

───────────────

The next morning I woke up before dawn and got dressed. It was a beautiful warm Saturday morning in late July. It was July 26 to be exact. I wore light blue jean cutoffs and a pink tank top that had Sassoon written on it. Steve met me somewhere in the city. I was impressed he got up so early. I wondered if he had done that so he didn't have to explain why I came to his house so early. I wondered if he had told anyone at all. We drove to the clinic in silence and I prayed there would be no protestors or well-meaning Christians outside.

We made it in without a scene and were in the clinic elevator. My heart was racing. I knew that this was a big deal. I knew that this was a sin. I feared the real possibility of eternal hell. The elevators doors opened. The fear was thick in the air. I don't know the name of the clinic, or the doctor or even what town we were in. A nurse met us in the first room.

"He can't come any further," she said nodding toward Steve.

"Oh, okay," I mumbled. "You have to stay here," I said turning to him and shrugging.

He half smiled and hugged me.

"Okay, I'm ready," I said to the nurse.

She took me to an inner waiting room where there was a television and children. Who would bring children to an abortion clinic? Yes, cartoons on the TV and children. No one looked at each other. I sat with my head down, my mind was racing. I knew the Lord but I did not know I could talk to Him. I thought about what Father Eaton had said but heaven seemed to be closed that day. I sat in silence and fear and waited for them to call my name.

Eventually a nurse opened the back door.

"Suzanne…" she called my name. I'm not even sure I used my real name and nobody asked to see any identification or proof of my age, nothing. The nurse took me into the back room. It was so cold, so very cold and I could hear the hum of some sort of generators or fans. I did not look at anyone's face. I believe it was partitioned off with curtains. We walked through the big concrete room.

There I was again on the thin wire between life and death. I wasn't sure if I was alive, I wasn't sure if anyone was alive. The rooms were filled with death. *Was I walking through other people's abortions behind those curtains? Were lives just floating all around and up through the ceiling?* I tried to clear my thoughts, to turn them off, but the death was so loud.

The procedure is very cloudy in my mind. There was a monitor turned away from me and a sheet between me and the doctor. I'm not even sure if it was an actual sheet or a sheet in my mind. I did not see him but a big piece of equipment on wheels accompanied the doctor's arrival. A nurse walked up next to my head and

I could see her waist. She reached for my hand under the sheet.

"It won't take long. Do you want me to stay with you?" she said softly as if she didn't want the doctor to hear. I nodded and I closed my eyes tight and endured the seconds ticking away.

"Really, it's ok, we do this all the time. It won't have any long term effect at all. I've had two," she said squeezing my hand. "You don't even have to tell anyone," she winked at me.

Too late for that, I thought. I was smarter than that but I wanted to believe it wouldn't have any long term effect on me. I heard an awful sucking sound. It was horrible. It is the only thing I clearly remember to this day. It changed with the physical pain I was experiencing. It was an incredible ache. Like an ache I had never even imagined nor experienced since. I forced myself not to imagine what was happening.

She was right, it didn't take long. As soon as the doctor was out of the room and the machine was wheeled behind a curtain the nurse gave me a friendly "tap tap" and I was told to sit up. She helped me back into the room with the cartoons on the TV and I waited there. I was numb and staring at the floor and soon I felt another tap on the shoulder.

"You can go Suzanne." I looked up, dazed. "You should stay in bed and use pads.

You'll probably get a fever and notice some bleeding. That's normal. Go to the emergency room if you hemorrhage, meaning if the bleeding gets very heavy, if it makes your bed wet."

"Oh," I said as I walked out into the outer lobby where Steve was waiting. He stood up without looking in my eyes and helped me into the elevator. He hugged me from behind. He was so sad. I think he was sorry but he never said it. We didn't say anything to each other at all. It was a heartbreaking moment. Neither one of us would ever be the same. We felt certain that what we had done was unforgiveable.

I dropped him off and drove home. I had never felt that feeling before, hollow. I remember hoping I didn't pass out while I drove but I was a very determined young woman and forced myself to believe this was not going to take me out. I told myself I would be unaffected by this day and that tomorrow I would wake up and life would go on. I was tough, after all.

I walked up the path to the front porch and my mum and dad were waiting there together arm in arm. They looked so scared and worried.

"Are you okay?" my mother asked. I nodded and walked past them.

"We will never have to talk about this again," she said warmly, trying to comfort me. She meant that they would not hold it over my head and I knew that but what I heard was that I had done the unspeakable and therefore we would not speak of it.

    I went to bed and she brought me something to eat. I slept for a long time, possibly days. I don't remember.

Chapter 5

I woke up from a light sleep. The rabbit was curled up under my arm. It was late summer and the evenings were very warm. The sun was setting but a warm breeze blew. The leaves were just beginning to lose their greenness. I knew we didn't have much time.

"Let's just stay here for a little while," I whispered.

"Tell me a story," he said sleepily.

"What kind of story?" I said.

"Tell me more about your life before." *He closed his eyes and looked content and nostalgic.*

"Before what?" *I said but I knew what he meant.*

"Before me." *His head was warm and his whiskers were tickling my arm.* "Do you remember before?"

"Of course I do. But, you're not a problem you know, I don't mind you. I'm used to having you around. It's not like it was so much better before." *He stared at me from his reclined position and his gaze narrowed.*

"You're lying," *he said piercing me with this his rabbit eyes.*

"Ok just a little while and then we have to go home."

"We'll both go home eventually," *he said.*

When I was 5 our family attended a little church called St. Christopher's. It is a big part of all of my childhood memories. Our family was very active in the church. It was our own little community. The building was small but had two stories and the sanctuary was all windows. The pews were actually individual wooden chairs with individual kneelers and each one had a red Book of Common Prayer and a hymnal. The downstairs housed all the classrooms and the Reverend's office.

It smelled like an Episcopal church, a mixture of candles and God. Outside was a brick wall we used to sit on after church and all the people would mill around smoking and drinking coffee.

My parents did Bible study every week at different homes. We went to every pancake supper and midnight Christmas Eve candle service, and I met Beth Ann. We were in Sunday school together and she is, to this day, my best friend for life. I have been very blessed in my life to have several "best friends" but she is like a sister. Having known me since I was 5, she knows my whole life. We love each other like sisters and we have fought like sisters, but we know we are "lifers".

Beth Ann however, knew nothing of the events of July 1986. This was the kind of dark secret you could not tell anyone, not anyone. By the fall of that year our relationship was strained by the gaping crevasse of my secret and I missed her dearly.

Steve and I continued to date throughout the next year. The following summer Steve left for Army basic training. It was one week before my high school graduation. I was miserable at the idea but I knew deep down that it was his way out.

A few days before he left I sat on the edge of my mother's bed. She was reading and looked up from her book. I laid my head on her chest and let out a big sigh.

"You aren't going to run away and get married are you?" she asked stroking my hair.

The question shocked me and I looked up at her. No one had ever suggested that, least of all Steve.

"No. I…well…just no," I said dropping my head back down. But I now questioned why Steve had never thought of that.

The time came for Steve to leave and I said goodbye to him somewhere in the city. We waited together for the recruiter's bus. There were a lot of people there and Steve was very detached. We said goodbye and he said he would write. My heart ached as he got on the bus. I watched the bus drive off and wondered what would happen to me now. We had definitely decided to stay together and do this long distance relationship so I knew it was going to be a long summer without him.

    Two weeks later I was set to graduate from high school. The morning of my graduation I drove into the city early. I wore a white linen dress with a big sparkly tiger on the front which tied at the thigh although the hem was at my knee. It's hard to imagine but I thought I looked pretty great in it. I had a speech to make and I was asked to be there early to oversee the set up. I was nervous and excited. The string quartet arrived and began warming up.

    It was a beautiful spring morning and the sun was shining. I wandered nervously around the beautiful courtyard somewhere in Shadyside and I could hear the faint sound of the string quartet. I felt sure my family would walk up the path at any moment.

    The rest of my graduating class arrived with their families. There were only about 15 of us but everyone was there now. Where was my family? We had no cell phones in those day and these kinds of things were just something you endured, not knowing. Expecting someone and just not knowing where they were was the most frustrating state of being. Thank God we don't have to deal with that anymore. I was standing in the garden in the sun when Bill, my English teacher came out into the garden.

"It's time," he said cheerfully. I craned my neck to the parking lot as I followed him into the hall. The ceremony began with a beautiful piece by Franz Schubert. I sat in my graduate seat, still no sign of my parents and my brother. The musicians finished and it was time for my speech. I took a deep breath and just as I stepped up to the microphone I saw sunlight coming through the door at the back. In they walked, well my mum and dad walked and my brother hobbled in on crutches.

I wanted to scream, "Where have you been?" but I remained poised and made my address to the Class of 1987.

We graduated together that beautiful spring afternoon, the 15 classmates of The Oakland School class of 1987. It was exciting. Everything seemed new and the world was full of wonderful adventure and possibilities.

We had a reception in the garden and I made my way through the crowd to my family.

"What did you do?" I asked my brother looking at his giant casted leg.

"I put it in the boat prop on Joe's boat," he said half smiling and half humbled by the pain and maybe a little bit of humiliation.

"I should have lost my whole foot," he said looking a bit amazed. I still, to this day, don't understand when or how that happened on my graduation morning.

The day after my graduation we went to England as a family. My mum, dad, brother and I were all born in England and frequently made the journey to see the rest of the family. We have lived in the United States since I was a baby but I have always felt very connected with England. My parents both had very strong English accents as I grew up. We had many English traditions and customs and of course, my grandparents, aunties and uncles and cousins were all there.

We were in the terminal waiting for the plane and I was watching my brother and my dad balance his crutches on their chins. They were giggling and challenging each other and it was a moment I will always remember. We were both now high school graduates and I was certain this would be our last family vacation. It was.

Chapter 6

Steve did write, all summer. I had a letter almost every week. It was early August when he finished basic training. His mother contacted me and told me she had bought a new car and invited me to go to see Steve's graduation. I was 18 by this point and was starting to really feel like an adult. I agreed excitedly and requested the time off from my pizza delivery job.

Steve's mother, his little sister and I drove all through the night. We arrived at the base the next morning and sat in the big bleachers in the baking sun. The platoons did their formations. They were very impressive. I couldn't pick him out for anything. They all looked exactly the same.

After the ceremony we moved through the thousands of soldiers and finally found Steve's platoon. I could hear his distinctive laugh and I ran up to him.

"Hi you!" I said.

He saluted me and my heart sank. "No PDA. Plus you're a civilian," he said militantly.

"Oh," I said stepping back. *Excuse me*, I thought. Apparently, hugging or any display of affection was strictly prohibited on the base.

He had leave to come home after the graduation ceremony and we drove the 14 hours home. He was very different than I remember, harder and very stern. I looked forward to him being himself again. That did not happen. Something was different. Something between us was missing.

A few weeks after Steve came home from basic training things were finally beginning to feel a bit more normal. I wasn't sure nor was he where he would be deployed but we both had hope for his future. It was a Saturday in July and I called him at his mother's house.

"Hey," he said. "I'm gonna spend the day with my boys."

"Ok, I have to work today anyway," I said defensively. "Should I come over after work?"

"Um yeah, I guess that would be okay," he said but really he didn't seem to care either way.

I worked the lunch shift at The Bellaria Pizzeria, Homemade Ice Cream and Smokehouse Ribs (quite a name and we had to answer the phone that way) and came home to the farmhouse. My Dad was waiting for me on the porch, his face was white.

"Steve's been wounded," he said gently moving toward me.

My heart began to race. *Wounded? How could he have been wounded, he was home on leave?*

"What do you mean?" I said through my incredible shock.

"I don't know any details. His mother called here. He's in the hospital. I'll drive you there okay?" he said.

"Okay," I said in a daze as I felt his warm arm around my shoulders.

It was dark and stormy as my father drove me on I-79. We found the hospital and once inside we went to the information counter and were told where to find Steve's room.

We walked in cautiously and he was lying in a hospital gown with many IV's. He looked more vulnerable than I had ever seen him in my life. He looked at me, half smiled and said "Beanie ran me over." I don't know Beanie's real name but I knew who meant.

"Why? How?" I asked moving slowly toward him.

"We were screwing around and I rolled off the hood. My foot… it's crushed." He looked down to his foot under the blanket. I was furious, sympathetic and then furious again.

"Does it hurt?" I asked knowing that was a stupid question.

"Yeah," Steve said nodding.

I stared into his eyes. I could tell he was fighting back tears. His face looked different. When he was accepted by the Army he had developed hope in his eyes. The hope was waning now.

My dad walked right to his bedside, laid a hand on his shoulder and began openly and boldly praying for Steve.

"Let's pray," he said the way he always did.

The room became silent all but the sound of his voice and Steve closed his eyes and he seemed to relax under my dad's touch. I reached out to touch his foot and he opened one eye as if to say please don't touch it. I was so proud of my dad that day. He was very fatherly to Steve, probably more fatherly than anyone had ever been to him and he seemed grateful. Despite what we had done, my dad treated Steve with respect and love. Dad finished his prayer and gave Steve's shoulder a squeeze.

"I'm being shipped to Bethesda Naval Hospital for reconstructive surgery. They're really not sure they can fix me," he said and his voice cracked. "The brass is not very happy with me for damaging government property," he said and I hugged him feeling his hospital gown. How scared he must have been. I think he was only 21.

Steve was shipped to Bethesda Naval Hospital and underwent reconstructive surgery. Sometime in late August I answered the phone in our farmhouse kitchen. It was late at night and the voice said, "Collect call from Bethesda Naval Hospital."

"I'll accept," I said and I felt a rush of excitement.

"When are you coming to visit me?" I was excited and shocked to hear his voice.

"I'd have to drive to Maryland? I suppose I could…I suppose I would love to do that. I would have to ask. Do you **want me** to come see you?"

"Of course I do," he said and his laugh was warm and gentle.

I finished my phone call and ran into the television room. I gently suggested the idea to my mum and dad and they said they would think about it.

Later that evening I was summoned downstairs and they said I could go and offered to let me take my dad's Mustang because it would be safer. My dad's Mustang was the coolest car on the planet and I excitedly agreed to that "safer" plan. They also insisted I take someone with me so I called Beth Ann and of course she agreed.

I got up early the following Saturday morning and put on my favorite white mini and a blousy peach, off the shoulder top. I felt great in it. I picked up Beth and we made the journey all the way to Maryland without incident.

It was around lunchtime when we arrived and I found a parking space in the huge parking lot. I was proud of myself for negotiating the traffic around Washington DC and felt very capable. The hospital had a glass front and a reception desk in the big, glass atrium. A woman helped us locate Steve's room and we made our way to his floor. I could hear his laughter and banter as we went down the hall and finally into his door.

"Well it's about time!" he joked and laughed as we came in obviously for the benefit of his roommate. He gave us both a hug from his reclined position and was genuinely really happy to have us there. There was a very fit, very solider-like nurse in his room.

"He's only allowed R&R for 2 hours. Don't bring him back late ladies, or there will be big trouble."

"Oh, we won't be late," we assured him and helped Steve with his crutches.

We got him in the car without too much trouble and we went to Pizza Hut. It was so great to be together and one of the best memories of our relationship. The doctors were cautious but hopeful that he would recover and be able to march again. That was the defining issue, whether or not he could march again. Our time was very short but we also knew we had to leave for the long ride home so we took him back to Bethesda.

He gave me a warm kiss and hug goodbye in the lobby.

"I can take it from here. I'll be home soon," he kissed my forehead like I was a child and swung around on his crutches.

"I'll be FINE!" he said looking back at me. I stood and watched him as he hobbled into the elevator and the door closed. Beth Ann and I strode back to the car and began the long drive back to Pittsburgh.

Sometime in the night I began to get sleepy and giddy and Beth Ann and I were giggling and speaking in loud English accents and carrying on as we always did. Suddenly, she became sad.

"What is it?" I said turning off the radio.

"I know I'm being stupid but Candy's sick," she said breaking down. Her family cat was getting old and sick and she knew it wouldn't be long and she would be gone. It is quite symbolic of youth slipping away when your childhood pets begin to die of old age. She was so vulnerable and honest about how she felt and we talked a long time about Candy and life and death and how unfair it is that we have to lose those we love.

I suddenly felt a tug in my heart to tell her. I suddenly felt like it was time to tell her what I had done.

"Ok, so I have to tell you something." I started. She was silent so I continued. "You know last summer when I met Steve?"

"Uh huh," she said guardedly.

"We…well I, got um…well I got pregnant." I figured I just had to say it. She was still silent. I was staring at the road and trying to keep my thoughts straight and the car between the lines.

"So…I, uh well… I couldn't face it I just got scared and I went to a clinic…and… I never thought…I couldn't have a baby could I?" My thoughts were scattered. "Well I just didn't know what to do. I couldn't find a way out." My words sounded completely foreign and they hung in the air. I wanted to suck them back into my mouth.

I looked over at her in the dark with the orange glow of the dashboard light and she had huge tears in her eyes.

"Pull over," she cried. "Pull over!" She was pleading now. I did as she said this time and pulled onto the shoulder. She and I sat on that highway shoulder and cried and cried and held each other for what may have been an hour. She held my face in her hands.

"Why didn't you tell me?" she sobbed. "I would have been there for you." I had no answer for her.

"I couldn't tell anyone but my parents," I replied. We cried some more.

"Don't ever do that again!" she said half laughing and half crying. "Don't keep things from me." We hugged again and dried our tears. We began to gather our wits.

"Give me half," she said, which is what we used to say to each other when either one of us was sad or in pain. We spent a long time on the side of that highway that night but the world continued to speed by and we were frozen in time.

Chapter 7

"We should go, it will be dark soon," I said stroking his head. "We don't want to be out here all alone in the dark."

He looked up at the sun perched to descend over Old Orchard Hill. "It's pretty, isn't it?" he said.

"Yep. It really is."

"You should see it from my perspective." he said absently.

"As a rabbit?" I asked. "Does the sunset look different to a rabbit?"

"You could say that." He looked right at me. His gray nose quivered and his eyes were glossy like two marbles.

"Come on, we have to go."

Just then a brown baby rabbit suddenly emerged from the long grass and stood on the edge of the blanket. He looked startled to see us and stood perfectly still with just a quivering nose. The three of us were all completely motionless and silent. After an uncomfortable amount of time, I opened my mouth and took a deep breath.

"Hi, I'm Suzie, would you like to…" the baby bunny turned and bolted off into the long grass.

The rabbit let out a loud exhale and a chuckle. "That was not your finest moment," he said laughing at me.

"I thought he was..." I threw my head back and laughed so loud it echoed through the orchard. "He's not like you."

"No, he's not 'like me," he said pointing at his zipper. I leaned forward and uncrossed my legs to get up.

"Hey um," he stammered. "Why don't you just leave me here and go on home? I'm fine." He looked at me hopefully and I furrowed my brow. Eventually he dropped his head.

"It was worth a shot. You're going to hold onto me forever aren't you?" he asked and I looked down at him.

"Of course I am. Who else is going to hold you?" I said scooping him up and cradling him.

A few weeks after our road trip to Bethesda Steve finally came home from the hospital. I was so excited that he would be around again. I hadn't been able to talk to him much, but I was looking forward to catching up and getting our relationship back on track.

I had to work the day he was scheduled to arrive, but I knew he wouldn't be home until late morning. I got up early and busied myself until I thought he was home. I dialed his number from the phone in my bedroom. I was sitting on the edge of my bed wearing my red pizza delivery T-shirt and black leggings. The phone rang several times.

"Hello?" he said.

"HEY!" I said excited to hear his voice.

"Hey," he said very unenthusiastically.

"Should I come over after work?" I asked rocking back and forth on my bedside.

"I don't think I'll be here. Me and some of the guys are doing something," he said.

"Oh." My heart was sinking. "How about tomorrow?" I asked. He let out a big sigh.

"I don't know, probably not." I was trying to figure out what in the world I had done. He was clearly breaking up with me and I was clueless as to why.

"Steve, what's going on?" I said quietly.

"Nothing, I gotta go." Click.

I felt nauseas and stunned. I hung up the phone and made my way downstairs. I walked numbly down the front path and climbed into my VW. I sat behind the wheel for a few minutes. It'll be okay, I told myself. It's probably the shock of coming home. He'll call me tomorrow. I went to work. He didn't call.

I was delivering pizza somewhere near Passavant Hospital the next day and I stopped to use the payphone. It was a sunny, fall day and I stepped inside the phone booth. The door was missing but the phone seemed to be okay. I put my quarter in and dialed his number. His mother answered and then I heard her shouting for him to pick up.

"Hey," he said as usual.

"Hey," this time it was me who was flat. "So, do you want to see me?" I asked. There was a long silence.

"What's going on, Steve?" I was getting mad but my heart was aching in my chest.

"I can't be a soldier, Suzie. I can't march again and they probably aren't taking me back," he said.

"That's ok," I said hopefully. "You still have me." There was silence again.

"I have nothing to offer you. You have a life to live and what am I going to offer you?" he said eventually.

"Steve, I don't care about that stuff."

"Yeah, well I do," He said quietly and then he was gone. The dial tone blared through the earpiece.

I pictured him hobbling into the elevator in Bethesda and turning to smile as the doors closed. That would be the last time I would ever see him. The pain was unbearable. I walked back to my car and sat and cried in the parking lot for a long time.

Suddenly I could smell the pizza on the backseat and I snapped back into reality, realizing that it was getting cold and I was about to lose my tip. I wiped my tears on my sleeve and reached down to get my keys. Just then I felt something soft and furry in my lap. I looked down to see a big, furry, dark gray rabbit.

"Where did you come from?" I whispered, cradling him like a baby. He was motionless and heavier than he looked. His legs were limp and floppy and I noticed he had a zipper.

"What's this?" I whispered touching his zipper. "Did you get hurt?" I felt his soft belly and noticed some dried blood around the zipper like the wound was fresh.

"You'll be ok," I said as I cuddled him and rocked him. I stroked his long grey ears. They were soft and limp like his legs. His eyes were closed and I traced around his soft, little face with my finger. His whiskers were long and black. I pulled him close to my face and listened for breath. I couldn't seem to hear his breath so I blew on him and his fur moved and his eyelashes.

"There you go," I said as I touched his little, gray nose. A few of my tears had dropped onto his eyelids and I dabbed them dry.

"Sorry about that," I laughed through my tears. "You'll be okay now," I said but I had a fleeting sensation of that wire I had become so familiar with. That life and death wire and a chill seemed to blow through my car. *Why did I feel that way?* I looked again at his zipper. I wasn't sure how a live rabbit could have a zipper but he felt good in my arms like a baby. I stabilized his limp neck. I had always held our cats like that and he, like our cats did not protest.

"I'll take care of you," I said. "You just stay right here with me." I positioned him carefully on my lap so that my hands were free to shift. It felt right. Yes, I was going to keep him forever.

Chapter 8

I woke up the following day late in the morning. I opened my eyes and stared at the ceiling. The ache in my heart had moved to my belly and I realized I was hungry. I turned my head to see my rabbit on the pillow next to me. I reached over and stroked his head.

"We should eat," I said quietly as I pulled him in to me. I made my way down to the kitchen. The sun was beaming brightly through the big windows and the fall leaves were in full splendor.

"Good morning dear," she said as my mum appeared from the laundry room. "I thought you were going to sleep all day." She was staring at me and I protectively covered my rabbit.

"Are you alright?" she said noticing my trepidation.

"I'm fine," I mumbled as I opened the fridge and poked around. "There's nothing in there," I said closing the door.

"There are plenty of things in there," I could hear her patience waning. "Are you sure you're alright?"

"Yes! I'm fine! Geez Mum maybe I'm just tired. Did you ever think of that? Maybe since my boyfriend dumped me I'm not very chatty. Ok?" I said clutching my rabbit to my chest.

"Ok, there's no need to snap at me. I'm sorry to hear that but it's not the end of the world, Suzie. You might not see that now…"

"Ugh!" I groaned aggressively, turned and walked out. I did not want to hear about how she'd had her heart broken when she was my age. She didn't seem to be holding a rabbit and I doubted anything she had to say was going to help me feel better. I had to get away from her.

I stormed up to my bedroom and flung myself face down on my bed. Rolling over I placed my rabbit on my chest as tears ran down my cheeks onto my pillow. I stared at him. "Where did you come from?" I said stroking his face. *Now that I had him what was I going to do with him?*

"I suppose now it's just you and me," I said resigning to my new role as his mother.

"Let's get out of here," I said and put on some clothes. I carefully stuffed my rabbit up under my sweatshirt and bounded down the stairs.

"I'm leaving!" I shouted. There was no reply.

I really had no idea what I wanted to do with my life. I was only 18. I continued to work at The Bellaria Pizzeria…etcetera while I nursed my broken heart. Julie had moved to Florida and Beth Ann had moved to Youngstown and was going to Youngstown State University. I would drive to Youngstown on the weekends and hang out with her and her college friends. We had a lot of freedom and she was, after all, my best friend and we just liked hanging out doing nothing, which we did frequently.

The following weekend, as usual I drove to Youngstown. I thought it would be good for me and my rabbit to get away and get over Steve. My rabbit was strapped in next to me and I was also just happy to get away from anyone who would ask me if I was ok. I was so sick of that question. Did I look ok? Did anyone look ok holding a zippered rabbit?

I came to a secluded part of highway. I was still in the farmlands of Pennsylvania and therefore, everything looked familiar. I was getting a bit sleepy with the sun on my shoulders and was shaking my head to stay awake. Suddenly out of the corner of my eye I saw something. It was big and golden. It moved very quickly across the road and startled me.

"Good Lord, that was a lion." I said to myself.

I looked over at my rabbit seat belted beside me and I feared for his life for a moment. I remembered once as a child I had seen what looked like a lion in a field near our house. I told my mother and she told me there were rumors about mountain lions in western Pennsylvania. The lion I had seen then was not a mountain lion and the one I had just seen was not either. "King of the Jungle" lions were unheard of in Pennsylvania and so I put it out of my head. *Must have been a deer*, I thought to myself and looked for an exit so I could buy a Diet Coke and snap out of my drowsy hallucinatory state. *Why did that lion look so familiar?*

There was excessive partying going on in those days and this weekend was no exception. It all seemed quite innocent but looking back I can see that we were all indulging in some pretty dangerous behavior. My rabbit went with me to every party. I didn't think anyone else could see him. I drank heavily keeping the rabbit stuffed up under my shirt most of the time. I forgot all about the lion on the highway.

I wasn't going anywhere on the path I was on so the second semester of 1988 I moved to Youngstown and enrolled at YSU. I think my mum was glad to see me go. I wasn't very nice to be around. My parents and Beth's parents shared the cost of our apartment, and Beth worked at Arby's and earned our beer money for penny draft night. She hated working there and eventually she managed to get us both jobs at the Reading Lab. I still don't know what we were supposed to be doing there. Answering the phone I think. It was a fun time, I suppose. Looking back I wouldn't want to live that lifestyle again but when you are 19 it feels right.

There was a fraternity house nearby and we became "little sisters". If you are reading this and have daughters or you know anyone who has a daughter, discourage them from pledging to become anyone's little sister. It was degrading and disgusting.

We lived in a big, old green house on the north side of Youngstown. We had the whole bottom floor but the kitchen was tiny. I had the back bedroom and we had sliding pocket doors which made Beth's room and a front room with a fireplace. It was plenty for us and we really liked it there. Beth Ann and I spent a great deal of time at campus bars, even though I was underage. We made friends with various bouncers and people who would let us in. We thought we were having fun, we really did.

We would spend our days in class and our nights, at least Wednesday through Sunday in the bar. I took my rabbit always and people seemed to stay away from me because of him. It actually didn't take long to get really old. The nightlife had its charm but we would rather spend most our time giggling in our apartment.

One particular afternoon we had gone to the mall and Burger King. Burger King and McDonalds factored quite highly on the priority list. We always made sure we had $3.07 after a night of drinking for what we called "The full meal deal": Big Mac, large fry, Diet Coke. That afternoon we were returning from the mall in my little VW rabbit.

"Hurry, I have to pee!" Beth said her voice straining.

"Me too!" I said and we started to giggle. We consumed copious amount of Diet Coke and were frequently desperate to pee. We were straining to get home, each claiming we had to go worse than the other one and it was clearly going to be a race. We pulled into the driveway which was on a slight grade and scrambled out of the car in a pushing, shoving, all out race for the bathroom.

"I'm first!"

"No, I'm first!" We shouted pushing and running. I don't know which one got there first. We each got our turn and it isn't relevant. Once relieved of our burden we were resuming our afternoon of frivolity when we walked out onto the porch of the big, green house. Beth noticed a car in the yard across the street.

"Hey, somebody has the same car as you," she said pointing to the car that was in the yard, on the grass, next to a telephone pole, very close to a telephone pole actually. We both shrugged and focused our attention toward our own driveway. We stood in shock as there was no car where we had left it. Most people drove a standard back then and well, I really had to pee and apparently did not put the car back in gear. We did a double take to the car across the street and burst out into fits and giggles which still happen to this day if we talk about it. We ran, giggling all the way to the car, jumped in and sped off before anyone could question our ability to function as adults in the real world.

Beth and I spent many afternoons lying on the bed or sofa just talking. I would lie on the couch with my rabbit and we would just pass the time in each other's company. I wasn't worried about Beth seeing him so it was a relief to be behind closed doors with her. She never mentioned him but I knew she could see him. She accepted that I had him and that he went everywhere with us. We had no cable back then and there was no one we would rather talk to so we just talked to each other. It was a simple and yet very deep relationship.

Beth Ann had struggled with her weight ever since she was a child. I didn't care either way but I knew it was something she hated about herself. It also made her a target for jerks. I think if she were thin I would have felt differently about my rabbit being out in the open. Beth was very approachable because she was overweight. It made her seem flawed and accessible. From time to time she would look right at him, but she never asked about him. I was grateful for that. I did not know where he had come from so I certainly didn't know what I would say if she did.

One warm night in November Beth and I walked together across town to a fraternity party. It was very crowded that night and the mayhem seemed to have no end. I was sitting at a small, homemade bar in the basement when one of the senior brothers started to talk to me. It was dark except for the glow of a black light. The music was incredibly loud and I could hardly hear him but he was giving me shot after shot of tequila. Things were very fuzzy and I was somewhat dizzy. He was very handsome but his face was distorted and he had many eyes. He was smiling at me.

"I want to show you my room," he shouted into my ear.

"Your room?" I shouted back.

"It's at the very top. You'll see," he shouted again and this time grabbed my hand pulling me off balance from the barstool.

"Whoa," he said steadying me. He was smiling and he seemed nice. I looked around quickly for Beth but I didn't see her.
"My friend…" I said.

"We'll come right back," he shouted with his mouth very close to my ear.

He pulled me through the crowd. It was very dark, very crowded and very loud but he had a tight hold on my hand and I couldn't slow down if I wanted to. Once we shoved our way through the throngs of people, we got to the back stairwell and I could hear only ringing in my ears. I was stumbling but he kept pulling.

"Come on, it's not much further," he said towing me up the winding stairs. My rabbit was under my arm but I was losing my grip and I feared I might drop him.

"Slow down," I said trying to get my footing.

Once we got to the top he pulled a key out of his pocket and opened a very big, heavy door. We entered the room which had a giant bed which was perfectly made with a bright blue bedspread. Many trophies and ribbons were all over the walls. The room was immaculate and there was a huge skylight which revealed all the stars.

"Wow, this is amazing," I said sitting on the edge of the bed for fear I might fall over and looking up at the skylight. He sat down next to me and looked at my lap. I pulled my rabbit closer. He reached to my lap and gently tugged on him. Suddenly I could feel him on top of me. My rabbit had fallen and I couldn't reach him.

"Stop it," I said and pushed on his chest. He was much bigger than me. I heard a thud of something hitting the floor.

"STOP!" I shouted and this time I was really struggling. My squirming didn't help and I finally reached between us and pushed on his face. He let out a big, disgusted sigh and suddenly stood up.

"Stupid tease," he said and he reached down to the floor and picked up my rabbit.

"I dated a girl who had one of these before. She was a stupid, crazy bitch too." He had my rabbit by the throat and I was frozen in fear.

"Don't, you'll hurt him!" I cried.

"Get out you crazy bitch!" he hissed and threw my rabbit at me. He opened the door and I ran out almost falling down the stairs. I ran through the crowded halls, pushing past all the drunken partiers.

I ran out the front door of the fraternity house and kept running all the way across the north side of Youngstown. It was the middle of the night and I could hear my rapid, staggered breath as I ran. I had nothing in my hands but my rabbit but I felt safer than I did in that frat house. I reached our apartment and put the key in the lock but the door was already unlocked. I ran in looking for Beth.

"Beth?" I called out for her frantically. "Are you here?" Then I noticed the light coming from under the bathroom door and I could hear her crying. I threw the door open and she was on the floor. I slumped down next to her and we hugged each other tight. Her eyes were as red and swollen as mine. I noticed her shirt was torn.

"I couldn't find you," she said looking at me with her big, green, bloodshot eyes.

"I know," I said hanging my head. "Are you ok?"

She nodded. "Are you?" I nodded back.

"No more fraternity parties?" I half laughed and half cried.

"No more fraternity parties," she said as we held each other tight on the bathroom floor.

Chapter 9

The rabbit was zipped up inside my sweatshirt as I hiked down the old trail.

"What do you think people think of me?" he said with his head poking out above the zipper.

"What do I care what people think?" It was somewhat true.

"You care," he said knowingly.

"You're mine. It's you and me. If they don't like it they can piss off."

"Charming language," he scoffed. "I just think you make things hard on yourself when you take me places. It might be easier…and people might find you more likeable if it was just you…you know without a zippered rabbit."

"I don't care if people like me or not. I don't need anyone…period," I retorted.

"Yes you do."

"Oh shut up, would you?" I said shoving his head down my shirt and reaching for the gate at the bottom of the trail.

The next few months of 1988 we avoided the fraternity house and kept ourselves in the bars with new rules about leaving each other alone. One night in July we had plans to go to penny draft night at the local campus bar. I was reclining on my bed, stroking my rabbit and didn't feel like getting ready. Beth was inside her closet looking for something to wear.

"I don't really feel like going tonight," I said lazily. She didn't like that statement at all.

"Come on! You have to go, she said from inside the closet.

"It's always the same," I said. "It's getting boring."

"I know," she said and popped her head out. "But seriously, are we just going to sit here and do nothing?" she raised one eyebrow looking at my rabbit. "Go on, take a shower. You'll feel better after that. I'll let you wear my jean jacket and I'll curl the back of your hair," she grinned hopefully.

"Oh fine," I submitted and went to the shower.

We arrived at Pogo's Pub that night and Beth and I were sitting in front of the taps. We liked to sit there. There was a bartender there whose name escapes me but he looked like Michael Bolton a bit and he was very nice. He showed a little bit of interest in me and so I enjoyed his company but I wasn't really interested.

It was business as usual. The regulars were coming in and Beth and I camped out for the night at the bar with our smokes and our penny drafts. I was facing the stage and Beth was facing me. Suddenly I could see something had caught her attention. Her eyes lit up and she looked at me knowingly. She kicked my leg gently.

"A guy just walked in who looks just like Sylvester Stallone." Her eyes were on me but her head was pointing to the door. I knew that she was pointing him out solely for my benefit because I was a big Sly fan and everyone knew it, especially Beth Ann.

I turned coolly and calmly to look toward the door and sure enough there he was. He was absolutely beautiful, big brown eyes, a bit of stubble, scruffy black, curly hair. I couldn't look away. There he was and he was looking straight back at me. Our eyes locked for a moment and I felt my heart skip a beat. I had to look away because it was a little awkward but I also didn't want him to think I wasn't interested. I kept the gaze a moment or two longer, looked back once, looked down at my rabbit and back at Beth. I was so cool. I was so calm. I was so flushed!

I gave Beth one of those *Oh my God* faces. She smiled and we continued to talk and try to look nonchalant. It wasn't long and I saw him again, making his way to the bar.

I stared at Beth with eyes full of, *I can't believe this. He's coming this way.*

She stared back as if to say, *No way!*

We had a whole code of looks that we knew by heart and if you've ever had a best friend you know what I mean.

This beautiful man, this man who made me breathless, walked right up to me. There was no mistake he was there to talk to me. He looked me straight in the eye.

"Hi, my friend wants to leave but I just couldn't leave without saying hello." My mouth was dry, my hands were clammy. I sipped my penny draft.

"What's your name?"

"Tony," he said.

"Of course it is what else would it be? You look like a Tony." I felt stupid.

"And your name is?" he raised his eyebrows.

"Oh yeah... oh, it's Suzie." I shoved my rabbit behind me and stumbled over my own name.

He stayed there and talked to me for a long time. His friend, the one who wanted to leave, came up several times and Tony sent him away, several times. Eventually they stepped away from earshot, had a conversation and his friend left. Tony was still standing right next to me. Beth had gone off to dance or talk to someone and he sat down with me. I don't remember what we talked about really. My rabbit was still shoved behind me on the stool but I wondered if he could see him.

I know I lied about my age; I know he told me he was Italian and that he wanted to be a teacher. We talked and talked and the bar became more and more crowded. When you sit in front of the taps you get shoved together but I didn't mind. Every time a group would belly up to the bar we got shoved together again. We had been there for quite some time.

"I don't usually do this but I really want to kiss you," he said into my closest ear.

I looked him square in the eye. It seemed I could see his warm soul through those big, brown eyes and I could see he meant me no harm.

"Go ahead then," I said as if to challenge him. He called my bluff and I saw actual fireworks. He smiled at me. The lights were suddenly genuinely flashing and we knew it was last call.

"I have to go check on my sister," he said reluctantly, holding both my hands. He had come out that night to keep an eye on her because she was having trouble with an old boyfriend. *Some eye he was keeping on her,* I thought but I wasn't complaining. I didn't want him to let go and certainly didn't want to say goodbye.

"Why don't you come by our apartment when you're done?" I blurted. I knew Beth would be there and I doubted he would take me up on it. I told him exactly where our apartment was.

"I'll just make sure she's ok and then I'll stop over," he said looking at me seriously.

Beth and I went home and we started making a huge pot of macaroni and cheese. The way the tiny kitchen was situated it overlooked the front stoop and we suddenly heard a knock on the old wooden, screen door and I saw a male shadow on the porch. We both did the *Oh my God!* face and I quickly turned off the mac and cheese. I ran and threw my rabbit on my bed and ran back to the living room. I calmly opened the door. There he stood in our doorway. I couldn't believe it. I really didn't think he would actually show up!

We sat up talking and eventually Beth Ann went to bed. Tony and I talked until the sun rose and he suggested breakfast. We were both starving as I had abandoned the mac and cheese. Beth was still asleep so we sneaked out and went to Perkins. I had some kind of Italian omelet and Tony had Eggs Benedict. I remember the cheese was very stringy and it was very hard to look cool while I ate. I did my best but left most of it on the plate.

When I got home that morning I was so overwhelmed. I crawled into bed. He said he would call and if that was true I just had one sleep and the phone would ring. Just one sleep, if I could sleep. I finally did manage to fall asleep and woke up to Beth sitting on my bed.

"So…what happened?" she asked excitedly. That was the first of a million questions and answers.

"He's Italian and he wants to be a teacher," I said falling back onto my pillow.

"You're all dreamy." She giggled.
"Dreamy and hungry!" I said.

We made some food and dragged our bedclothes out the backdoor to the small patch of lawn between the house and the driveway. There we set up camp to sunbathe and discuss the events of the night before. I had also dragged out the phone which was connected to a long landline. He said he would call and I was not going to miss that.

We were enjoying our lazy afternoon and the sun on our faces, among other parts of us when the phone suddenly and unmistakably rang with that old rotary phone ring. We did "the face". There were a couple more rings and I coolly and calmly answered.

"Hello?"

"Hi…Suzie?" It was him!

"Yeah, oh…hi," I said

I cuddled the receiver hanging on his every word while Beth rolled around giggling on the ground.

"I really had a great time last night and I can't stop thinking about you. There's a fireworks show tonight in Youngstown. I was wondering if you might want to go. It's called City Fest. Have you heard of it?"

"Um, yes I think so. " I had no idea but I wanted to go. I smacked Beth on the back trying to silence her.

"I'll pick you up at 6 ok?"

"Ok. Bye then," I said trying to contain myself. I hung up the receiver, paused and flung myself, squealing onto the ground joining Beth Ann.

I got ready that night paying attention to every detail. Beth helped me pick out an outfit from the few dressy items I had. I meticulously applied my makeup and she curled my hair. It was almost 6 and my heart was pounding.

"Do I look ok?" I said twirling.

"Of course you do," she said handing me my purse. "Now come on!" I knew she wanted to get to the front room so we could secretly watch out the window for his car. I excitedly stepped out through the bedroom door and turned off the bedroom light with a click. Darkness fell on my rabbit lying on the bed all alone.

The next I knew we were sitting on the hood of his car watching fireworks. It had been 24 hours since I had first encountered this man and I was a flood of emotion. I was not sure what I was getting myself into but at least at that moment I was willing to keep going.

Chapter 10

The next few months were absolutely amazing. Tony called every day and took me out almost every night. We could not stand to be away from each other. It was summer, the nights were beautiful, I was falling in love and I hadn't carried my rabbit in weeks.

We really did some fun things that summer. Tony took me to my first adult concert. It was Meatloaf and it was outdoors. I loved being with him so much. He held my hand everywhere we went. He was so kind and gentle. It was a whole new world.

Late that summer my parents sold our farmhouse. I knew I had to go and say goodbye and I took Tony with me for support. They were just loading up the last moving truck when we arrived. I didn't pack one box. I didn't help them move. I don't know why not. We stood in the driveway and looked up at the house.

"Well I guess that's that," I said irreverently.

"You ok?" Tony said putting his arm around me.

"Yep. Let's just go ok?" I said feeling the need to run away from there.

"So, we are going to the new house?" he said encouragingly.

"Yes, the new place." I climbed into the car noticing my rabbit on the seat.

"Oh there you are." I said quietly sliding him between the seat and door. I had not seen him in a while and I was not exactly happy he was there.

"I hope my Dad has some beer there."

"I'm sure he does," Tony chuckled.

"Let's get some just in case," I said quite seriously.

"We're in PA we'd have to buy a whole case."

"Oh well," I said sarcastically.

"Oh, okay," he said hearing my tone and knowing I was not old enough to buy beer for myself in Pennsylvania.

By that fall the crime rate on the north side had increased and our parents were worried about our safety. Because of this Beth and I also moved that summer. We moved into an apartment building across the street where most of the YSU baseball team lived. They pretty much ignored us. We weren't exactly their type and Tony was ever present.

One morning Beth and I were making breakfast. She had not been herself lately and our relationship was feeling distant.

"You ok?" I asked her over the breakfast table.

"Not really," she said pushing her hash browns around on her plate. "You're never around anymore." I could see the pain in her eyes.

"I know. I'm sorry," I said. "But it's hard because of Tony," I said sympathetically but somewhat defensively.

"I'm late," she said looking at her plate.

My stomach flipped. There was a long silence.

"Oh no. How late?" I asked. This was too familiar.

Suddenly she jumped up from the table and ran to the bathroom. I could hear her retching and I followed her in. Rubbing her back I did not know what to say. I felt so guilty because I had not been true to our rules of never being alone with a guy. I felt guilty because I had spent so much time with Tony. I felt so protective of her but that was counter balanced by the compulsion to run from the apartment. I handled it very clumsily.

    Several days later Beth and I went to a Christian pregnancy center on Market Street for a test. I wasn't allowed to go in with her. We went to Burger King afterwards and she looked deeply into my eyes. "I can't have an abortion." she said tenderly.

    I nodded silently.

    We came home and that night she and I sat on my bed.

    "I'm gonna have the baby," she whispered looking down. "There's never been any doubt if I really think about it. My parents are going to help me and I'll give it up for adoption."

    "Oh. Yes, that's a good plan. You're very brave," I said pulling her in for a hug. "I will be there every step of the way. You will not ever be alone. I'm so proud of you."

    We talked for a while about a birth plan and eventually she went to bed.

    I sat on my bed and felt very alone. I stood up and opened the chest where I had placed my rabbit. I pulled him out from among the clothes and cradled him in my arms. He had grown since I had last seen him earlier that summer. He was getting quite big now. I gently pulled on his zipper. It got caught a couple of times but I decided I needed to see what was inside. I exposed his entrails. They were not bloody, just wet and mostly grey and they smelled pretty bad. I pushed his guts around as if I thought there should be more. There were no signs of life.

Tony and I were spending even more time together at this point. He was the best thing that had ever happened to me and he seemed to accept me just how I was. He told me he loved me but it really scared me. I didn't say it back. In fact, I was often shocked by my own reaction to his affection.

Slowly I realized I had to tell him what I had done. I felt like the person he knew was a lie. He was way too good for me. I felt like it wasn't fair to lead him on at this time in his life when he didn't know who or what he was dealing with.

One night he came over and we sat in my bedroom. I had been drinking a lot that evening before he got there. I sat on my bed drenched in tears. The room was spinning and I was heartbroken because I thought this would be goodbye.

"I have something to show you," I sobbed. I went to my chest and pulled out my rabbit. He sat perfectly still. I placed my rabbit on his lap and stroked his head. He looked down at him.

"It's ok. Suzie," he said warmly.

"No, it isn't." I had to keep going and the alcohol seemed to help me press on numbly. I reached over onto his lap and unzipped the rabbit's zipper. "See?" I said looking at his guts.

Tony looked right at the guts. His face did not change and he did not look away.

"No, I don't see," he said now looking at me. *Couldn't he see his guts?* I thought.

He gently put my rabbit on the bed and gathered me up in his arms and I felt his scruffy beard on my cheek.

"I've known about him for a while Suz." He lifted my chin.

"You have?" I said.

"Yes, I have." He held me tight and I pulled my rabbit into our hug. We were safe there. I never wanted him to us go.

———————————

Several months later Beth moved home to Pittsburgh. She never told me this but I would imagine she didn't want to go to YSU once she began to show. It made sense to me and still does. My parents moved me into a little studio apartment in Hubbard where Tony had grown up. It was a little bit lonely in there. It was in the basement level and I had never lived alone before. Tony was there quite a lot and took good care of me during that time. He bought me my very first ever television set. It was Christmas and I remember thinking he must be pretty serious about me to buy me a TV for Christmas.

Beth and I still saw each other as much as possible and we each drove back and forth from Pittsburgh to Youngstown. I was Beth's Lamaze coach and considered myself the baby's father. I really did. The last few weeks we attended Lamaze classes at Passavant Hospital and I learned a great deal about fetal development. My rabbit grew by leaps and bounds in that environment. Beth had made solid plans with an adoption agency and there was a family all picked out waiting for their new daughter. It was all so well considered, planned and intentional. I was so proud of her.

It was May 16th when I got the call.

"It's time," she said. "I think my water broke. We're going to the hospital."

"I'm on my way. I'll meet you there."

My heart was racing as I ran to the parking lot, got in my VW and started to drive to Pittsburgh. I felt very alone in that car that day. My Mum and Dad, as I remember it, were in England and I suddenly felt very young, inexperienced and scared. What if this was not the right thing? What if she was supposed to keep this baby? We were so young, what did we know? I began to reflect on the faith-filled way I was raised as I started my journey. I began to remember my mum and dad praying whenever there was a big issue in their lives. My heart saw a glimmer of hope as I drove onto the overpass on I-680.

"Well Jesus…" I said as I turned off the radio. "If you really are there and you really are God, I need you now," I said audibly. I felt silly but I was desperate. "Beth's gonna have a baby, but I guess you know that already," I continued. "She's gonna give her up for adoption and Lord, I know that she would listen to me if I told her not to do it." I was quite boldly speaking now. "So, I need to know Lord, if this is the right thing. If she is supposed to give her daughter away….I mean, is this in your plan?"

I stared up at the sky above the road and suddenly there was someone sitting next to me. I didn't look at Him but I knew He was there. As clearly as you can sense a human being sitting next you, I could sense that He was there. He told me it was His plan for her to give

Amanda up for adoption. He told me it was the right thing. He also told me that I was going to look back on that day later in my life and think that I was imagining Him, but that He was real. He was really there and He loved us both very much.

    I couldn't wait to tell her and I excitedly pulled into the parking lot at the hospital. I ran into the hospital carrying my rabbit in my ever growing purse and found Beth's room. I saw her in a hospital bed for the first time, and I could not believe this was about to happen. She was wearing a hospital gown and her big belly was covered by a sheet. She sat up and looked at me with a bright fluorescent light shining above her head.

    "Hey," I said smiling with my head cocked. Her eyes searched mine. "I have to tell you something." She sat up even more. "God was in my car, Jesus Himself. He said you are doing the right thing. He said He loves us both very much, and He said everything is going to be ok."

    "Really?" she said wincing from the pain.

    "Yes, really," I said squeezing her hand.

    She seemed comforted by this news but she was in a lot of pain. We tried to draw on our Lamaze training. I was wearing a neon pink t-shirt with some kind of abstract picture on the front. I told her to focus on the design to get through the contractions. We breathed together, we made small talk, and the afternoon dragged on.

It was hours. She would get frustrated with me and I knew she was in real pain, pain neither one of us had ever experience before. Beth's mother and her sister were in the room too and we all waited together. Every so often a nurse would come in and check on her but basically we just spent the afternoon breathing and waiting. Eventually a nurse came in and took us out in the hall.

"Beth's labor is not productive enough and her hips are too narrow for the baby to get through." She looked very serious. "They are preparing an operating room for a C-Section. Would you like to tell her?" She was looking right at me.

"Oh yeah. Ok, I will." I said realizing that I was the "father". This was suddenly getting even more serious and even scarier. I went back into the room.

"Hey." I whispered. "They want to go in and get the baby surgically."

"Oh." She said nodding. "Ok then." She took the news quite well. "I'm scared but I'm ready for this to be over." She said with a few accompanying tears.

We prayed together and waited for the news that the O.R. was ready.

Shortly thereafter several nurses came into the room.

"The operating room is a sterile environment and we always try to minimize any risk so only fathers are allowed in," one of them said. I frowned at Beth and then hugged her.

"I will be right here when you come back." I said and I held her hand as they wheeled her out. I sat down and cried.

About 10 minutes later the door unexpectedly opened and our favorite nurse was there looking quite excited. She grabbed my hand, pulled me up and handed me a paper gown. She was covering my head and shoes with plastic bags.

"I'm an adoptive Mommy," she said "and I think what you girls are doing here today is so brave and she needs you by her side in there. But you have to hurry."

My heart was racing as she escorted me through a closet-like room and through another door. When I popped out the other side there was Beth, well just her head. She looked up at me upside down and smiled.

"What are they doing?" she asked quietly. A big, green sheet separated her from the surgeon.

"They are getting the baby out," I said like it was a secret.

"Would you look and see?" She asked.

"I don't want to," I whispered. "I think I would see your insides." She nodded dreamily and smiled.

I sat on the little stool right near her head and stroked her forehead.

"Can we talk about something else?" she asked. My eyes got wide and I smiled under my mask.

"Well sure." I tried to think of something, anything to talk about. "What classes did you sign up for next semester?" Just as she was forming an answer I heard the doctor.

"Someone has been eating their Wheaties," he said.

Suddenly, Beth's whole body moved violently toward the curtain. I tried to hold onto her as her head moved south. Then I heard a loud suction noise and she popped back up where she had been. She stared at me with her eyes wide.

"Can you see her?" She asked. I stood up from the stool momentarily and saw the baby.

"Yes, she's here," I whispered. We were both crying as we stared, wide eyed at each other. Slowly Beth closed her eyes and drifted off to sleep. I could hear the baby crying on the other side of the sheet. I stared at the sheet between baby and mother. That sheet looked familiar and suddenly I felt very alone.

Chapter 11

It was the next day or the day after that the plans were made to relinquish the baby. Beth had to stay 48 hours, which is longer than usual, because she had a fever. Her parents, Beth, and I were waiting in her room. One of her parents was holding the baby and I remember her Dad was crying. The social worker arrived and we all looked at each other.

"It's time sweetheart," she said and Beth's face became distorted with pain. She took a deep breath.

"You do it first." She fought back tears handing me the little, pink bundle. I carefully set my rabbit on the brown, vinyl covered hospital chair and received Amanda in my arms. She was warmer than my rabbit and she wriggled and breathed. I looked at her little face.

"Well you, I hope I see you again someday." I kissed her right on the middle of her forehead and savored her smell. It was hard to let go, but I handed her to Beth's mom and she did the same, then to her dad, and then to Beth. We all kissed her on exactly the same place on her forehead as if it had more potency if we did it that way. I stood back and watched Beth Ann hand over her daughter. It was the most unnatural act I had ever witnessed. The social worker rather quickly turned and walked out of the room. Beth collapsed into a heap on the floor. It was as if she had no bones and no life in her body. I ran to her, gathered her and lifted her up. Her dad was looking out the window with his back to us and her mother was curled over in the chair. I held her to my chest as she was slumped over on the side of the bed. Her body was shuddering. I could feel the pain as if it was heat radiating off her body.

"Give me half," I whispered and she sunk into my chest.

We stayed together in that room for a while and not a word was spoken. It was much later that afternoon when she got her discharge orders and was finally free to leave.

Her baby was safe and on her way to her new family, Beth's pregnancy was over, and a nurse told us we were free to go. We walked out together with our arms around Beth and just as we did, I reached back to the chair without looking and snatched up my rabbit.

Chapter 12

I opened the big steel gate and closed it with a loud clang. I marched up the old path which was like a long tunnel of greenery teeming with crickets and grasshoppers and gnats. I swatted at the bugs as I carried my picnic basket. I continued past the hay barn and up the second tier of the enormous hill. Once I reached the top I took a deep breath and gazed out across the open field, nothing but hilltop and sky. Ah finally, I thought.

I unpacked my blanket and pillow and smoothed the blanket corners. Sitting cross legged I reached into my picnic basket and pulled out an IC Light. Popping the top I smelled that first smell of ice cold beer than made all my senses come alive.

"You drink a lot of beer," said the rabbit.
"You say a lot of words," I said sipping my beer.
"Have you always drank that much?"
"You know the answer to that."
"Why then?" he said imposingly.
"I'm not talking about this with you," I said calmly.
He lay on the blanket and stared at me. "You know the way you keep opening me up and looking inside," he said.
I paused and sighed. "I'm just checking on you," I said, "to see if you're okay."

"That's what hurts, he said. "That's why I bleed. You have to stop looking inside."
I touched his soft head, and stroked his ears, and looked at the dried blood around his zipper.

"Am I doing that to you?" I asked.

"No," he said, "you're doing it to yourself. It's just that you don't bleed...not on the outside."

"I'm okay," I assured him.

"You haven't been okay since the day I met you," said the rabbit. He sat up and wiggled his ears at me. "What were you really like," he asked, "before I came along?"

"Normal I guess," I said. "I was just a normal kid. I didn't have any baggage that's for sure, not until you came along. I told you I was just normal, nothing special."

"Yup," he said, "that's what I thought. Just a normal kid, and now you're stuck with me." He hopped onto the edge of the blanket. "You're sure special now," he said sarcastically.

"I like you," I assured him.

"You don't just like me," he said. "You love me."

"Not when you're all bloody and telling me it's my fault," I pushed gently on his little soft chest. I was beginning to get angry with him, sitting there with his big accusing eyes.

"Can't you just go away and be like any other kind of rabbit?" I said finishing my first beer and crushing the can in the middle.

He hopped away a couple of feet, and I was afraid he was leaving.

"Don't go!" He looked back at me as if I were overreacting.
"I'm right here," he sighed settling down onto the very edge of the blanket.

Tony and I had been dating for a little over a year, and Beth and I had a new apartment on Hillview Avenue. We had all grown up over that year and a half, and although things weren't always perfect we still loved each other very much.

Beth had met a new guy. His name was Kurt and they were soon quite an item. I was so happy for her although I think there was a part of me that was jealous. I had always been the focus of her attention and although I had Tony now, I still wanted her to need me. We had somewhat separate lives although we lived together. I was involved with Tony and his friends in Hubbard, and Beth was involved with Kurt and all their friends from work.

One night Tony and I went for a drive. Although I had an apartment to sit in and he had whole house to occupy, we decided to go park behind Sharon Steel. We drove around the back of the parking lot where it was very dark and climbed up on the hood of his car. We were reclining there looking at the stars and making idle conversation. I was holding my rabbit at my side when it suddenly got very cold. I didn't say anything at first but wondered if he felt it. Then

I began to sense a presence. I think we are equipped by God to sense other beings and when it happens it's unmistakable. I got a chill all through my body and I tried to pretend I was fine. Just then, Tony looked over at me with a look of concern on his face. We stared at each other for a moment as the wind began to pick up and became louder.

"Do you feel that?" he asked.

"Yes, I don't want to stay here," I replied shivering. We scrambled into the car and sped out of the parking lot into the street lit up with light poles.

"What do you think that was?" I asked nervously.

"Not what it was, but who," he answered staring straight ahead. From that moment I knew that God had a reason for us to be together. It was a great comfort to my soul that Tony seemed to be able to sense what was good and what was not. I knew that we would do great things together and that not everyone was happy about it.

Chapter 13

I was working as a bank teller in those days. Tony was a union carpenter, simple yet honest work. One Friday Tony called me at work and said he wanted to take me out to dinner. I was game but thought we should go somewhere affordable, ok cheap. We had, as I said, simple yet honest jobs. He told me he wanted to treat me to a fancy dinner and wanted me to wear my green dress.

That night he arrived at my apartment to take me out on our dinner date. I had ditched the green dress idea and was wearing a denim skirt and top. His shoulders dropped when he saw me.

"The *green* dress," he said.

"I just don't feel like a fancy dinner tonight. I feel fat and this is more comfortable," I whined. "Can't we just go to Rosile's for a shrimp basket?" I continued to whine as he shook his head.

"Please, Suzie for me?" he pleaded with those big brown eyes.

"Fine!" I stomped off half seriously to my room and put on the stupid, green dress. We arrived at Alberini's restaurant which I knew to be the finest Italian restaurant in the area.

"We can't afford this," I said as we pulled into the parking lot.

"Shh, I just want to do this ok?" he said smiling at me his eyes wide and hopeful.

"Ugh, fine," I said as I flopped my rabbit up and down on my lap with great exaggeration.

Once inside the restaurant I was unable to enjoy the atmosphere. I just could not get comfortable with the idea of this big, fancy dinner on our wages. A hostess came and escorted us to a table in the middle of the room with big, fancy high back chairs. We were seated and the wine steward brought us the wine list.

"I just want a Screwdriver," I said. Tony furrowed his brow, but gently.

"Let's just get a bottle of something red."

I stared back at him defiantly. "Wine gives me a headache," I insisted.

"Ok, bring her a Screwdriver but also bring us a bottle of Cabernet," he said to the steward politely.

The waiter arrived with the dinner menus and we sat quietly as I stared at the prices. Every so often I would look over the menu to see if Tony was alarmed by the prices. He was not.

"We should both have this pasta," he said pointing to a name I could not pronounce. "Linguini Con Fruitti De Mar," he said sounding it out. It was scallops, shrimp and clams in a marinara over linguini and sounded good to me.

"Ok, that looks good," I said. I was starting to relax and enjoy myself by this point.

The vodka in my Screwdriver was doing an excellent job. The waiter came and took our order and we sat back taking in the place. I reached for my drink and noticed Tony fumbling with the inside pocket of his jacket. I tried to watch him calmly but became concerned with his fumbling. He looked at me with his eyes quite big.

"I'll be right back," he said and off he went. *Great, he's forgotten his wallet, this is just great.* I thought to myself. He wasn't gone long which was comforting and I settled in.

"Everything okay?" I asked.

'Yes fine, just fine," he answered. Tony poured me some wine just as our meals arrived.

"This is so romantic," I said to him. "Just like Lady and the Tramp"

"Hmmm…Lady and the Tramp huh?" he said twirling his pasta. "So, if I was going to ask you to marry me, would you want me to rent Lady and the Tramp and have spaghetti or would you rather I just said, you know, would you marry me, pass the salt?" I looked at him confused.

"I don't know." *What a weird thing to say,* I thought to myself.

Suddenly, Tony stood up. My eyes were as wide as can be.

''Suzie…" he said and he got down on one knee. I don't know what else he said because I was crying and blubbering

"What are you doing?" I said through my tears.

I was able to make out the proposal and my head was spinning. He took my hand and was placing a ring on it. My rabbit was right in the way and I tried to shove him to the back of the chair. I looked down at Tony knelt down on the floor, looking up at me with those big, brown eyes. *Had he forgotten? Had he lost his mind? Who would want to marry me and my rabbit?*

I stared at him and the tears just ran. I searched myself for just enough courage to throw out that lifeline. That line I knew would change everything. If I could just say it I know he would rescue me. If I could just say it I would be safe forever. I didn't deserve him and he certainly didn't 'deserve' me, but I couldn't speak so I threw my arms around his neck and my rabbit flopped onto the floor. He stood up and hugged me.

"Is that a yes?" he asked with tears in his eyes.

"Yes!" I blurted and there was a thundering round of applause in the restaurant and apparently a Catholic Priest was at a nearby table and he was blessing us loudly in Latin.

"It's not real is it?" I asked.

"Of course it is," Tony said holding me tight. I tried to sit down but couldn't.

"We have to get out of here!" I said crying excitedly, grabbing my purse and shoving my rabbit in it. We left our food on the table. I had to tell Beth! I had to tell my parents! I had to tell the world that I was getting married!

Chapter 14

There was a pile of beer cans in the grass by midafternoon.

"Is there any food in that basket?" the rabbit inquired. I looked at him somewhat glassy eyed.

"I've got some carrots for you," I said slurring my words. "You want some, sweetheart?" I leaned toward him nearly losing my balance. He hopped carefully onto my lap and looked at me warily as I gently fed him a carrot.

"Do you have any food for yourself?" He asked searching my eyes while munching on the carrot.

"I don't want any food," I lied. "I'm fine."

"You keep telling everyone you're fine."

"I'm FINE!" I yelled getting angry. "I keep telling everyone I'm fine because I am fine." I tried to lower my voice.

"If YOU had a zipper I could look inside and see how empty it is in there." He leaned his head against my belly. I reached down and stroked his soft grey head.

"Maybe it should be empty in there," I said gently. "I'm really okay, Baby. Don't worry about me. Everyone is always worrying about me. Just eat something they say…." I was getting sleepy and his soft fur was so comforting.

"Don't drink any more beer." He looked up at me and his nose twitched. "You're going to carry me down the hill."

"Oh yeah, how do you know? What if I left you here?" I said feeling a false sense of beer infused courage.

"You won't," he said.

"I could do it. You watch me….stupid talking rabbit." I stood up stumbling and sloppily scooped up my blanket. "I don't need you!" I said scornfully and continued stumbling down the hill,

"Bye!" I called over my shoulder as I left him sitting all alone in the long grass.

Tony took me to my parents' house the next day in his company's van. It was gold and I was sitting up high in the front seat. Tony had already admitted that my folks already knew. He had asked my dad a day or so before he proposed. We pulled into the driveway of their new house, and they were both standing out on the front doorstep, grinning.

My Mum later told me that my dad was telling people we were engaged before Tony even proposed and she jokingly asked him what would happen if I didn't say yes.

"Of course, she'll say yes," he said and he was right.

My Mum and I were headed to England on March 18, 1990. I had requested a trip to do some family searching, and my parents had always done all they could to get us back to England to see our family there. I've now come to realize that we saw our grandparents, aunties and uncles and cousins as often, if not more often, than most of my friends with American relatives. I'm grateful for those many trips.

We boarded the plane. I had checked my rabbit with my luggage, and the only thing I remember carrying on the plane was that ring on my finger. I sat in my seat and caught the light from the sun in the diamond and made it dance on the ceiling. I had learned in the previous 48 hours that it was indeed a real diamond and that Tony had picked it out and had been paying on it for months before he asked me. I felt so valuable with that ring on my finger. If any hijackers thought they were getting my ring they had another thing coming.

Our trip to England was so very exciting and I was able to share my excitement with all our family everywhere we went. I felt like I had a real future. The beginning of our engagement was one of the happiest times of my life.

Of course Beth was my Maid of Honor, I'm not sure I even asked her. It was understood. We decided we should get in shape for the wedding and joined a health club. We worked out early in the morning and changed our eating habits. My rabbit had gotten really fat and we both needed some work.

Somehow along the way Beth and I both lost control of that process. Beth became bulimic and I became anorexic. It was sort of symbolic looking back. She had too much and I had nothing. Sometime in those days I replaced food with alcohol. I began to really like the feeling of my empty stomach. That emptiness somehow felt normal and the alcohol helped me to feel emotions. I started to lie about my food intake. It seemed the less I ate the smaller my rabbit got and it made it easier to hide him.

A few people became concerned about my weight. I swore up and down I was eating enough, but they weren't buying it. I had to eat in front of people but I was afraid to gain. I had read somewhere that laxatives help you lose weight, so I started to secretly take them. It was not a nice way to live. The laxatives made me feel so sick that I couldn't go anywhere, and I would lie on the couch for hours. I would sleep until I could function again, until someone expected me to eat, and then I would start the cycle again.

My menstrual cycle disappeared sometime in the winter of 1990. I didn't really think about it. I think I was glad. One day the realization happened; I knew it would eventually. I realized that I was not going to be getting married and I was finally going to get what I deserved. One afternoon I asked Tony for a hug and he was unhappy with me.

"I'm afraid I'm going to break you, Suz," he said hugging me gently. I hugged him back and pulled him tight with my head on his chest. I felt his heartbeat and I knew I was going to die.

Chapter 15

My breath was erratic and panicky as I ran up the hill past the old barn. My legs and lungs were burning as I reached the clearing at the top. I fell on my knees and felt around in the long grass.

"Where are you?" I cried with increasing urgency. "Where are you? I'm so sorry! Please come out!" I felt all around in the long grass looking for a burrow. I thought about the foxes and hawks I had seen, and Holly…oh no, our dog Holly! How long had I been gone? Where was he?

"Please Baby! I'm here! Please come out!" I cried feeling and searching, the stiff thistle and wheat scratching up my legs and hands.

"I'm so sorry I left you," I said dejectedly and finally fell from my hands and knees, landing face down in the long grass.

"I'm here," he whispered and I looked up through the strands of hay and wheat to see the silhouette of his perfect, little, gray face.

"You're here!" I said sitting up and scooping him up with great relief.

"Of course I'm here." He looked at me and his eyes were warm and familiar.

"I'm so sorry, were you scared? I will never leave you again," I promised hugging him tight and cradling him in my arms. He wiggled free and hopped down out of my arms and sat a few feet from me. He nibbled on a long peace of green grass which

had shot up out of the wheat. He looked at me for a long time.

"I wasn't scared," he paused. "I don't stay here you know," he said mumbling with his mouth full.

"What do you mean?"

"I mean I don't sleep out here in a field at night with the foxes and the badgers and the fleas if that's what you think."

"You...you don't?" He munched and watched me. "Where do you go?" I asked. "Where do you sleep? Where do you go if I don't carry you?" He looked up at the sky. The clouds were big and billowy and there was a hawk circling.

"It's ok the hawks won't bother you with me here," I said reassuringly.

"I don't worry about hawks," he said continuing to look at the sky. The long blade of grass wiggled back and forth poking out of his mouth as his whiskers twitched. "Or badgers or fleas or dogs..."

"But who takes care of you when I don't?" I asked.

"I'm fine." He settled back on his haunches. "I'm better than fine."

"Now, you sound like me," I said leaning back and putting a long blade of grass in my mouth.

"It's not like that," he said wiggling his nose.

"Because you're dead?" He looked at me for a long time.

"Because I don't need you anymore," I felt a pain in the pit of my stomach. "I'm very well cared for...but, perhaps it's you who needs me," he lowered

his head and moved forward hopping onto my very thin leg. "You don't take very good care of yourself."

"Don't be ridiculous. What would I need you for?" I ignored his second comment.

"Maybe it makes you feel better, if you carry me? Do you feel better when you carry me?"

*"No, I feel awful when I carry you." I looked up at the sky. "But you know what? I think I deserve to feel awful. Maybe I deserve to have **my** zipper ripped open and my insides poked at. Maybe someone should pull out **my** ovaries." He didn't say anything and I looked over to see if he was still there. "If I did have a zipper I could open it up and put something in there and I wouldn't feel so empty."*

"Well you don't have a zipper." He paused. "But you do have a mouth."

"Don't start that again," I said looking at the fall apples on the trees." But I was hungry, very hungry.

It was March 1991. Tony treated me like a princess. He was more than I deserved and his affection was overwhelming. The guilt of his affection was so confusing. I almost felt like I was searching for a way out, for him…a way to set him free.

One afternoon I called Tony to come over. I had something to tell him. He arrived on time as usual and I sat down at the kitchen table. He suddenly looked worried.

"What?" he said cautiously

"I have to do something," I said. "And you're not going to like it."

"Go on, whatever it is, it'll be ok," he said gently reaching for my hand.

"If we're going to get married…" His eyes narrowed.

"If?" he interrupted and his voice sounded angry.

"Let me finish…if we are going to get married I want a clean slate."

"What does that mean?"

"It means Steve and I had unfinished business."

"And?" Tony's soft, big, brown eyes looked hard.

"And…" I continued "if that's the case I have to find him and say goodbye."

"Are you kidding me?" He was angry. "You're going to see that jerk? You don't owe him anything. He broke your heart, Suzie."

"I know." I tried to stay strong to stand up for myself. "But I want to marry you with a clean slate," I continued. "No regrets."

"Do you have regrets?" He tilted his head as if this was new information.

"Not about us," I said reaching for his hand. "I've never had any regrets about us."

He stared at the table and neither one of us so much as breathed. He glanced at my rabbit on the edge of table and took a deep breath. "Is this about him?" his tone softened.

"I think it might be." I pulled my rabbit protectively into me.

"Geez Suz, he's not going to help you with him." he said exasperated. "I don't mind him, you know that. I love you just the way you are."

"I know you do and I don't deserve how much you love me."

He stood up and pulled me into his chest.

"I don't want you to do this to yourself," he said with his chin on my head. "But if you have to…I'll go with you. I'll protect you."

"I have to do this on my own Honey," His face looked sad and worried. "I know you don't like it, but you can't stop me." It sounded familiar, like I had heard that somewhere before. I was once again determined to do something destructive and no one was going to stop me.

"I want you to be happy. I want to make you happy for the rest of your life." He lifted my chin. "And if this is something you have to do I won't stop you, but if he so much as touches you I swear I'll go there…"

"Stop. It's not like that," I said putting my arms around his chest and squeezing him as if to quiet him. "I just have to say goodbye." He reached one arm out of our embrace.

"I hope so," he said touching my rabbit on the table and sighing.

I still remembered Steve's number by heart and I called his house. His mother answered and she sounded surprised to hear from me. I don't think he ever told her anything to be honest. She called down to him like she always did and he picked up the receiver.

"Hey stranger," he said quite pleasantly.

"Hey…um, I will be coming into the city tomorrow and wondered if I could see you," I said nervously, staring at my engagement ring.

"Yeah sure," he replied.

"I'll come to your house about 7 and we can go for a drink or something," I said. I was 21 now and quite enjoyed that "going for a drink" line.

I drove to the city after work and walked into the apartment compound where he lived. In the past I had always come in the back, basement door which meant going through a little wooded path from the parking lot, but this time I entered from the street and walked up the front path. I felt different, grown up and really nervous. I walked up the big, stone front stairs and knocked on the unfamiliar wooden door. It was huge and I don't think I'd ever seen it before.

"What are you doing up there?" I heard a voice behind me. Just then, the front door opened and his mother Doris smiled a big smile.

"Well, hello stranger," she said enthusiastically.

"Well, are we going somewhere?" Steve yelled from the path. I gave Doris a quick hug, shrugged at her and trotted down the stairs.

"Hey," I said.

"Hey." We hugged. He felt around my jacket and within the first seconds of our meeting he reached in my pocket, pulled out my cigarettes and crushed them.

"Still smoking, huh?" he laughed. "Not tonight, muahaha!" He made an evil laugh. *Oh yes, I remember you now,* I thought to myself.

We walked down the street. 'What do you want to do?" he asked.

"I thought we would go for a drink somewhere," I said maturely.

"Oh so you drink now do you?" *Man, he made me feel stupid.* I thought. He had always made me feel stupid but I guess but I never really saw it.

"Yeah, I guess I do drink now," I said defensively.

"Ok, we can go in here." He turned into a little doorway and I followed.

The place was very crowded and very well lit. I was always uncomfortable in a bar with bright lights. In Youngstown we like our bars dark. We ordered a couple of beers and found our way to a booth.

"So, what's new?" he asked sipping his beer.

"Well, I am living in Ohio now," I said nervously.

"Oh yeah?" he replied and I didn't really think he was listening. "So are you going to kiss me or what?" He was laughing and fidgeting and I knew he was not paying any attention.

"No, I'm not….look Steve, the reason I wanted to see you…" He took my beer and put it on the table next to us.

"I'm not giving you your beer back until you kiss me." I was really starting to regret this meeting.

"The thing is…"

"No kiss no beer." I felt his face close to mine and I tried to move away, but his lips touched my face. His lips felt unfamiliar and cold, completely foreign and different than Tony's warm, soft lips.

"Steve, I'm getting married." I blurted awkwardly. His face dropped and he recovered quickly.

"Oh yeah?" he said, not handing me my beer. "Well, I still want a kiss." I looked down at my engagement ring resting on my rabbit that was looking quite sickly that day.

"…so, I just wanted to make sure there was nothing left between us…before I did it, before I said my wedding vows…"

"Like, what between us?" he asked but now he seemed to be listening.

"Like, I don't know," I said throwing my rabbit on the table. "I don't even know why we broke up. I just wanted to make sure there was nothing left you wanted to say to me." He looked at me quite serious now and his eyes were warmer.

"Look….um…I," he began. There was a very long, uncomfortable pause. "How long do you think you will be married?" The words just fell out of his mouth.

"What?" I said indignantly taking my rabbit back off the table. I stared at him. "Forever, Steve. If I get married it's forever."

We sat in that booth for a little while longer. He looked uncomfortable and we tried not to look at each other.

"Let's get out of here." he said and we slid out of the booth. We left the bar and walked slowly down the sidewalk.

"Let's go to my house."

"No Steve…" I stared at him.

"I won't try anything, I promise," he said convincingly.

"Just for a minute," I said reluctantly. We walked slowly and eventually through the familiar basement back door where he lived and he sat on the couch. It was exactly how I remember. I stood looking around remembering every detail.

"Just sit here for a minute." he said and patted the couch. I touched my engagement ring and positioned my rabbit carefully as I sat down. He really did not look well, my rabbit that is. We just sat there in silence. I could not believe he wasn't even going to acknowledge my rabbit. I looked at him searching his face. I wasn't sure what I was looking for, but I was searching for something.

"You're going to have to kiss me goodbye. You're not married yet," he said quietly. I felt his lips barely touch mine. I missed Tony more in that instant than I had ever missed anyone in my life.

"Steve, I can't…" I pushed him away.

"It's ok, just stay here with me," he said. Sitting back on the couch he let out a sigh and looked up at the ceiling. We sat there in that room in silence and eventually we both fell asleep.

As I woke up I suddenly realized where I was. I jumped up and looked at Steve. He was asleep and had my rabbit on his lap. I ever so slowly and gently pulled my rabbit out of his sleeping grip. He started to wake up and looked at me.

"Are you leaving?" he asked, clearly looking at the rabbit dangling from my hand behind my leg.

"Yes, I have to go," I said, now zipping my rabbit up inside my jacket. He watched the rabbit disappear behind the zipper. He nodded.

"Suzie…" He looked at me seriously. "Eat something." I nodded back but doubted I would.

"Bye," I whispered very quietly. I turned and went out the basement door, down the path and out onto the sidewalk. I had left my car on the street with a meter and I hurried to find it. I got myself in the car before I burst into tears. I looked up through the waterworks to see a parking ticket was on the windshield. *Well, I deserve that at least*, I thought to myself. I reached out the window and pulled the ticket off. 2:20 a.m. Well, *no one can ever see that*, I thought throwing it into the wind. I pulled myself together and drove my VW out of Pittsburgh forever.

The sun was just beginning to come up and my contact lenses were as dry as could be. I could barely see and the roads were all so unfamiliar to me. I couldn't believe that I had forgotten my way around so quickly. I was crying and that helped to keep my lenses wet, but I knew I wouldn't make it all the way home. I was able to make out a sign to 79 north and took the onramp. I drove and cried and sat in horrible construction traffic. My eyes hurt so much at this point I could barely see. I took the exit to my parents' house. My Dad always had good contact lens stuff and I had no choice. Again, I was caught in traffic and thought I might never get there.

Finally, I pulled onto their road and down the driveway. *No cars. Thank God.* I walked in the front door and into my parents' bathroom. As I put the lens wetting solution in my eyes I caught myself in the mirror. I was a wreck. I stared at myself for a minute in disbelief. *How had I gotten here? What in the world was I doing?* I was so tired and knew it would be dangerous to drive the hour north to Youngstown in this state so I slipped down the stairs and into one of the spare bedrooms. I crawled, fully clothed into the big comfortable bed. My parents' beds were always so warm and comfortable with big comfy duvets and clean sheets. I put my head on the pillow, hugging my rabbit and went into a deep sleep.

I didn't know what time it was when I heard the door open. "Suz?" my mother said worriedly.

"Yes, it's me." I turned my head and looked at her.

"I saw your car…what are you doing here?" she said and her eyes searched mine. I rolled all the way over now and she came and sat on the bed.

"Oh mum," I sobbed and I told her all about what happened with Steve. She scooped me up in her arms.

"You are mixed up aren't you dear?" She was rocking me gently. "Does Tony know where you are?" I nodded into her chest. She sighed and put her chin on the top of my head. "You know, you don't have to get married. Just because the church is booked and the dress is bought, if you're not ready, you don't have to do it."

"I really want to marry Tony," my voice was muffled. I felt the relief in her body and she smiled.

Would you like some food?" she asked.

"Ok." I knew it would make her feel better if I ate.

After I had eaten my breakfast I got my stringy rabbit and continued my journey home. I pulled into the parking lot of my Hillview Apartment and dragged myself up the stairs. I was still exhausted and crawled straight into my bed. Soon I heard the bedroom door open and Tony sat on the bed. I sat up and hugged him. He hugged me back cautiously.

"Are you ok?" he asked quietly and I nodded.

"He better not have hurt you."

"No, he didn't."

"So we are still getting married in 7 weeks?"

"If you still want me," I nodded and he rocked me back and forth. "I'm so sorry, I don't know what I was thinking," I said lifting my head. He kissed me and smiled. His lips were so warm. I was reminded how much I really loved him. There was no one else for me.

Chapter 16

I strolled down the rolling path that cut down the middle of the giant field of hay and the rabbit hopped along next to me.

"Why do you only talk to me when we're here?" he asked looking up at me from the path. He was sitting in one of the two paths worn by a tractor tire and I was standing on the other.

"I could ask you the same thing," I said smiling down but I could see he was serious. "I don't know really," I thought for a minute. "I don't even know your name."

"You never gave me a name." He stared at me. "You really don't know who I am, do you?"

"I guess not," I said throwing my arms out in exaggerated frustration.

"Well, you must be pretty thick," he laughed.

"Gee thanks, that's just what I wanted to hear from a talking rabbit... with a zipper." I let out a nervous laugh, took a few steps and turned to him. "So what, now you're telling me you're God?"

"Yeah right, do I look like God to you?" He hopped a few feet ahead.

"You look like a rabbit to me." I stepped over into his tire tread.

"Seriously, why only here?" He plucked a piece of clover he'd spotted and chewed on it.

"I guess," I paused "I guess I feel like we are safe here," I said looking around at the open fields. "I used to come here when I was a child...often. I've

never seen a single other human here unless I brought them with me. It feels close to God, with all the trees and the orchard and the open skies. It's the highest spot I know. It's sort of like heaven up here."

He let out an unintentional snort. "Um, no, not really... Oh, sorry... you're serious." He shook his head and his gray ears moved as if that would erase what he had said.

"Oh, so now you're a talking rabbit theologian?" I turned to walk back up the path. "Boy, I really am cracking up," I said running my hand through some long straw along the path.

"I said you never gave me a name!" he called from behind me.

"Your name... is Bugs!" I giggled and started to run ahead on the path.

"Bugs?" He stopped and thought hard "Oh, no, no," he laughed. I looked back and he was hot on my trail. I ran faster as he chased me.

The morning of our wedding was an absolute dream come true. The weather was a little chilly but it was bright. Beth and I got up at our usual 4:30 a.m., to head for the gym for a brutal workout on an empty stomach. We had our things gathered and were just about to leave.

"I can't go," I said to her suddenly.

"What do you mean? What's wrong?" she replied.

"I can't take any risks today. I have got to get married today or I won't be able to go on one more day." I was half kidding and half serious.

"You're serious?" she said.

"Oh yes, I'm serious, you go and I'll wait here for wedding time." She laughed at me and smiled.

"Ok, don't worry, I'll be right back," she said and gave me a big hug, and out she went.

I went into my room and pulled my rabbit out of my t-shirt drawer.

"You will need to be cleaned up for today," I said to him. I placed him in the bathroom sink and got the special bridal shampoo out of the shower. I washed him in warm water and towel dried him. I set the drier on low and fluffed his fur as I blew him dry. He was still gray and worn. I wished he was white just then. I held him in my arms. He smelled a lot better but he was still really skinny. I stared at his zipper.

"Not today, I'm not going to look in there today," I said knowing what I might see. I placed him in my bag with my spare pantyhose, my extra shoes and my can of hair spray.

Beth came back and soon my Mum and my bridesmaids were all there. They were making such a fuss over me and I felt like a princess. The limo arrived and we all headed to the church giggling and squealing all the way. We arrived at the church and my Dad helped me out of the limo. He stood back and looked at me.

"I expected you to look beautiful, but I had no idea you would look that beautiful," he said and I almost choked up but I held it together for my make up's sake.

The church was full and I have never been more excited in all my life. Everyone made their way down the aisle and then, it was our turn. My Dad gave me a wink and a "stand up straight" motion.

"Smiles everyone," he said like Mr. Rourke.

"I couldn't stop smiling if I wanted to, dad." He squeezed my hand.

"That's us," he whispered, hearing the organ cue and the doors opened. Tony was at the altar in a tuxedo. My Prince Charming was there waiting for me despite it all.

Chapter 17

We honeymooned in Jamaica and it was paradise. I barely took my rabbit out of the suitcase at all. They had a swim up pool bar, a human sized chess board, hot tubs and cold pools, restaurants, and a big wicker swan swing out on the pier. We tried to sleep in it one night and it was like sleeping on wicker, exactly. One afternoon Tony went out on a Sunfish and I nearly lost him for good. I was asleep in a chair when I heard a commotion. A crowd was gathering on the beach watching a Sunfish attempting to re-enter the harbor. A little Jamaican man finally dove in and swam out to bring Tony back in because he kept missing the break wall and the resort staff was getting concerned that he would drift out to sea. I made him promise not to do any more dangerous stuff. He reluctantly, but good-naturedly, agreed and we spent our days on the beach, our evenings in the piano bars and we planned out the next 60 years of our life.

When we returned from our honeymoon, we adapted to our married life. We had heard the first year is the hardest and I think we both agreed. Little things that would never even come up now were the center of much debate and tears. Still, we had no plans to turn back and knew that we loved each other and would get through the first awkward year.

One night in that first year we thought we would have a romantic night in our own very cozy home. The house was tiny but it was ours and I think our house payment was $125.00 per month. That night we went to Coca's Video and rented a VHS player. We had not "arrived" enough to have our own back then, and it was common for people to rent the whole machine. We rented the VHS player and chose a couple of movies. Fatal Attraction was one of them. We got home with our pizza and our movie and Tony set up the contraption which involved many cables and much swearing.

Finally, we cuddled up on the couch and began to watch this disturbing film. I was tempted to ask him to turn it off a couple of times but I didn't. It was just us and I thought it was grown up of us to watch a disturbing movie. Then we came to a scene involving a rabbit boiled on the stove. I remember recoiling at the site. The camera held on the boiled, dead rabbit. I asked Tony to pause the tape.

"Good", he said. "I have to pee anyway." He jumped up from the couch and went into the bathroom.

"Why is there a rabbit boiled on the stove?" I asked cautiously.

"Because she's pregnant," he shouted from the bathroom.

"What…," I stared at the paused scene. "Why?" I said in disbelief. My wheels were really spinning now.

"Yeah, you know the "rabbit died?" He was standing next to me now and looked at me as if I should know what this meant.

"Oh," I said looking down at my rabbit on my lap.

"Don't you remember that scene in MASH when they wanted to use Radar's rabbit to see if Hot Lips was pregnant?" he continued settling back in on the couch and putting his arm around me. *I do now,* I thought.

"So, the rabbit died?" I whispered. *That's why he said that! He couldn't even say the words…he couldn't say the word "pregnant". He never said it…never.* It seemed so clear now. Tony started the movie back up and I tried to comprehend what was happening but I don't think I followed the storyline much after that.

We watched another movie after Fatal Attraction but I don't remember what it was. I fell asleep and woke up to Tony trying to pick me up and carry me to bed.

"I will get up," I said sleepily but was unable to move. I looked down and my rabbit took up my whole lap. He was suddenly very heavy. He was upside down and sprawled across me and he was the size of a dog. I looked up at Tony and thought I saw a shadow of something moving in the kitchen.

"Come to bed," he whispered.

"What is that?" I said sleepily pointing to the kitchen. He smiled and pulled me up. It was a tufted tail, a tail of something with golden fur. If that was the tail of something it was a very, very big something. That night I had a dream.

I walked up the path to the old farmhouse. It was just as I had remembered only it had aged. It was very run down; my mind recollected every detail. I entered the front door and walked down the front hall, past the stairs and into the kitchen. It was musty and the floor creaked as I walked. I stood in the center of the kitchen and stared at the bright blue Formica table. It was peeling now and looked as if it might crumble. I looked ahead and saw the slatted door to the larder. It was coming off its hinges and I didn't open it for fear it would fall off. The chair rail was crumbling and there were chips of paint on the floor. I stood in that kitchen and longed for it to be back the way it used to be. I longed to hear the birds outside the Dutch door which we used to leave open at the top. I longed to hear the sound of the washing machine churning around the corner. I longed to hear the unmistakable sound of a car coming up the gravel driveway which signified someone who loved me coming home. I closed my eyes and imagined what it used to look like. My heart was aching.

Just then, I did hear a car. It was coming from the back which doesn't make any sense because the driveway was in the front. I walked back into the old laundry room and carefully opened the old rear Dutch door. There was a red Jeep Grand Cherokee parked in the yard. An old man got out and walked toward me. He was familiar to me but I couldn't place him. His face was stern but when he got closer it softened and his eyes became very warm.

"Oh, it's you," he said. "You come here every couple of years don't you?" I just stood and stared at him. I felt a need to defend my right to be there. It was MY old house, they were MY old memories. If he was going to tell me to leave he was going to get some resistance. He stood for a moment and looked up at the big old house.

"You really aren't supposed to be here, but I'm not going to make you leave, just don't stay too long." He said. I agreed and he got in his Jeep and disappeared into thin air.

I noticed an old bike leaning against the stone wall in the driveway and I got on it and rode off down the driveway. Suddenly everything became very unfamiliar. I began to panic fearing I would not be able to find my way back to the house. I peddled faster and faster and the sun was starting to set. Finally, the house came into my view. I ran up the front path and into the front door but this time, the old front door was slightly smaller.

I started up the stairs, covered in red carpet and they were very dusty. I reached the top and the old wrought iron railing was still there, the gate was open and I stood on the landing. I looked right and saw the old door to my bedroom. It was closed.

Ahead of me the door to my parents' old room was open so I went in. The bed was still there and still had bed clothes. Everything was very dusty and cobwebs were hanging all around the room.

I was just soaking it in when I looked over at the front window. I could see the big tree out front and the top of the barn, but then I noticed something. The window was shrinking. It was very slowly but very definitely shrinking. I felt torn. I ran to the landing and squatted and looked down the old stairs. The front door was now too small for me to fit through. I ran back into my parents' old room and around the bed. I was able to hold the window frame and stop the decrease momentarily.

I looked around the room and tried to savor the moment. I saw my mother's old dressing table recessed into the wall and I could see my own reflection in the big mirror. I was 17. I stared at myself and then quickly squeezed through the now, very small window. I climbed down off the roof and ran down the driveway.

I looked back quickly and the house was gone.

Chapter 18

Tony and I had never formally discussed the number of children we would have, but we knew we wanted children. My menstrual cycle had returned sometime during our first year of our marriage. I don't know how, but I had started to eat more normally. Tony prayed…a great deal about it. We had decided while we were on our honeymoon to use birth control for a while just to give ourselves time to adjust.

On our first year anniversary I decided to get Tony a puppy. That was a good start if we wanted to have children, a puppy! So, I was asking around regarding various litters I had heard of and dropping juicy hints to Tony. He was getting more and more intrigued by my hints. One night he walked into our tiny kitchen and slammed his hand on the table with a big smile.

"If you are getting me what I'm getting you, I don't think we want two so we had better tell each other."

"What?" I smiled.

"Is that true? If it's the same present we don't want two?" He scrunched his face like he didn't want to know. "On the count of three," he put his hand up, "one, two, three."

"It's a puppy!" we shouted in unison and burst into laughter. It was a funny moment and we were both relieved that we did not end up with two puppies. We both picked out Dauber from a litter from a friend's lab. His brother and sister in law also got a puppy from the same litter, and we spent a lot of time together with our dogs. He was really cute, brown and white, and he was a great dog. We considered him our first child for a while. He was a hunting dog but didn't seem to even know my rabbit existed.

Sometime during our second married year I decided it was time. I figured Tony was already on board, and I had always fantasized about that "surprise announcement" so I didn't tell him when I stopped using birth control. *It's a nice surprise right?* I thought. Well, the months went by and nothing. I was getting frustrated but still wanted to keep it a surprise so I didn't make my concerns known to Tony.

Eventually, after a year and a half I came to him. He was watching television after work with a bowl of soup on his lap. I sat down next to him. "We've been trying to get pregnant for over and year and nothing is happening." I said.

"We have?" he coughed practically choking on his soup. I remember wondering if he was secretly mad that I had kept it from him, but he was his usual tender, understanding self. "This is news…" he said as he searched my face.

"I know, I wasn't trying to be dishonest, I wanted a wonderful surprise, I wanted that moment." I felt the lump in my throat. "You know that moment, when I like put a pacifier in your lunchbox or something?" The tears streamed down my face.

"Oh *that* moment," he said as he pulled me in for a hug.

"Well, if you think we should get checked out, then we will," he said matter of factly. "Everything's fine, Suz," he said and lifted my chin. I hoped he was right and I carried my big rabbit into the bedroom to find the phone book.

We found a clinic nearby which specialized in infertility issues, and I went for my first appointment. The clinic had multiple forms for me to fill out. One of the forms asked if I had ever been pregnant before. *No,* I checked fearfully. The doctor was nice.

"How old are you? You just turned 24? Oh my yes, you have plenty of time to work this out," he said persuasively. "We'll do some preliminary diagnostic tests and make a plan."

He scheduled me for a hysterosalpingogram. It was the longest name of any procedure I had ever heard. It was basically an x-ray of the fallopian tubes and uterus. I went for my procedure and dragged my rabbit with me onto the exam table. I didn't look at the screen when the doctor was enthusiastically showing me my womb and all the various wonderful things about it. Instead, I unzipped my rabbit and looked around inside him. He was the same, just guts and entrails. I zipped him up and waited for it to be over.

"Everything looks good Suzanne," he said finally. "No blockages, no scar tissue. Your uterus is in working order." I let out a sigh of relief. *Now what?* I thought.

It was September 1994. We were told to "have relations" every other day for 3 months, an arrangement which made Tony quite happy. Still after 3 months we were not pregnant. The doctor decided he needed to get more aggressive and we had an in-vitro fertilization consultation. It sounded complicated, expensive and scary but we were both willing to do what was necessary. It involved many, many injections. Some of which, I gave myself in the stomach and some of which Tony had to give me. The drugs were intended to cause all my eggs to grow at once and then when they were all ready, I would get a big injection to cause my body to release them all at once and the doctor would harvest those eggs and inject them for fertilization.

The day of the procedure I was in an operating room and Tony was in an adjoining room separated by glass. It was bizarre and unnatural. The doctor explained that they had done something that would cause the eggs to glow so we could both watch the "miracle" on the screen. I held my rabbit as they wheeled me into the operating room. I directed my attention to the screen and watched as the weird, glow in the dark show continued. It was a strange feeling. Were we one second from life or a million miles away from it? It didn't take long and they took me to the recovery room.

Several weeks later they explained that we had three good zygotes and two iffy ones we could implant. We were scheduled to come in that Monday. On Sunday morning Tony and I were still in bed and our phone rang very early. Tony crawled out of bed and got the cordless, his face went white.

"Granddad?" He nodded and his eyes went straight to mine. I only had 2 granddads and one was already in heaven. I read Tony's face and immediately began to cry.

We drove to Pittsburgh and that afternoon my family made plans to fly to England to bury my Granddad. Of course, we could not go. I remember my mother said "We will go take care of the past. You stay here and take care of the future." It seemed wise and it made me feel important in the big picture. Grandchildren were, after all, our hope for the future.

We had decided long before the procedure that we would not freeze any embryos. If there were any of my embryos in this world again they would be inside me. They implanted all five and we were sent home with strict bed rest instructions. I ate Chinese food and watched movies for an entire week.

It was a tough week because I knew my granddad's funeral was going on, and I felt a lot of pressure to produce at least one baby at the end of all of this. But, I was amazingly peaceful. I had not spent much time stroking my rabbit that week.

It was 7 days since the implantation, we had our pregnancy test, and we were waiting for the phone call with the results. We had one cell phone between us and the clinic knew the number. Tony had taken the day off work to wait with me. We waited and waited and it seemed the phone was never going to ring.

"Let's go do something," he said feigning enthusiasm.

We decided to take a ride to the mall and look around. It had to be better than pacing the kitchen. We were strolling through the mall hand in hand when the cell phone rang. Tony held the phone up and motioned for me to put my head next to his.

"Hi, Tony?" I could just make out her words. It was Jen, our nurse.

"Yes, hi Jen," he said.

"I'm sorry Tony, the test is negative," I heard her say faintly. My body began to shake and I felt the darkness coming. Tony was hugging me.

"Thank you, Jen. Ok…yes… thank you….yes, I will…bye." He hung up and turned to me. "We'll just start again," he said. I buried my face in his chest, pressing my rabbit between us and let out a long, guttural groan. I had never heard myself make that sound before.

I pulled back to wipe my tears. Just then I felt something soft lifting my hand. He nudged my arm up onto his massive head. My hand slid down and I felt his mane and the power in his shoulder, and then my hand went back to my sleeping rabbit. The lion stood there staring straight at me, eye to eye. His eyes were the exact same color as his fur and his head was gigantic. I felt his breath on my face. I was frozen somewhere between fear and awe.

"Are you Him?" I whispered.

He looked down to the rabbit in my arms. I could now feel his breath on my hands as he slowly moved the rabbit as if to see if it was dead.

"He's mine." I whispered softly.

He closed his eyes and I heard a soft low growl. I let out a sigh of relief as the lion dropped his head and slowly moved on. He looked back just before he was out of view and stared into my eyes. His eyes were full of love. He swished his big tail and disappeared around the corner.

It took all the energy we had spiritually, mentally and physically to start over but we did. It was about this time that all our friends were having babies and it was rough. I avoided the baby showers and the church nursery. You can't take a big, sick, droopy rabbit to a baby shower and what would they think of him at church? No, I just avoided that altogether. We were in about week 3 when I was just beginning to feel "full" of eggs. The hormone shots were wreaking havoc on my emotions and my body, but I was clinging to the hope that it would all be worth it in the end.

Chapter 19

Fall was in full bloom on top of Old Orchard Hill. The trees were wonderful shades of orange, red and yellow, and the orchard below was so ripe you could smell the fruit even at the top of the hill. The field at the top had been cut and baled, and the whole place looked carefully groomed. It was still warm enough to be outside, and I was taking advantage of strolling in the afternoon sun.

"So," said the rabbit, "Am I the only one?" I stared at him with confused eyes. I raised my eyebrows.

"Only what? Only talking rabbit? Yes, you're my only talking rabbit." I said in disbelief. "You're the only one I need," I said softly.

"So…am I it forever? No more?" He asked as if he wasn't put off by my tone.

"What exactly are you asking me?" I leaned over and touched his nose patronizingly. He looked at me momentarily and then suddenly pulled away. His ears fell straight back. He stood up on his hind legs and his head darted back and forth.

"What?" I said looking around. "What's wrong?" Then I heard it, thunder. It was close. I felt a large drop of rain land on my head and then suddenly we could hear it softly landing all around us.

"The barn!" I shouted laughing and we began to run down the tractor path. The rabbit was faster than I had given him credit for. As we rounded the corner down the top tier of the hill the hay barn came

into sight. The rabbit disappeared under the door and I arrived just after him. I pulled up the big heavy door and scurried underneath. That barn was never locked. As I pulled the big door back down it rumbled the whole building. The sound was so loud and the rabbit hid.

"It's ok," I whispered. "Sorry about the door." The rain was pounding on the roof and siding which echoed loudly inside the barn. The rabbit peaked out from behind a bale of hay. He shook himself gently, and little drops of water flew in every direction from his fur.

"Come here. You're soaked." I pulled a blanket from a nail on the wall and picked him up wrapping him in the blanket.

"There. That's better," I said tipping him back onto his back and gently drying him. Just as I got to his belly he tightened up as if anticipating pain.

"It's ok; I'm not going to undo you anymore," I said reassuringly.

"You're healing," he said and smiled at me.

"If you say so," I replied continuing to stroke and dry his fur. "Now what's all this about you being the only one?"

It was a Wednesday evening when the phone rang. It was Jen from the clinic. "We're going to have to ask you to stop," she said. I felt like I was dreaming.

"What? Stop?" I was horrified. "There's something wrong with the heating/cooling unit at the clinic and we can't regulate the temperature to create the right environment for fertilization."

"How long will it take?" I said my heart pounding.

"We don't know. Suzie, we just don't know. Stop everything. Your body will reabsorb the eggs. We'll call you. Ok?"

"Ok." I was numb and she was gone. I sat down in our living room and looked at my rabbit on the chair. He looked sickly and not very cuddly. I was lost.

The next few weeks were some of the hardest weeks of my life. Tony and I held each other at night and cried. It was scary, but we had decided that if it was just going to be just us that was actually not so bad. We loved each other so much and there were so many people who couldn't even say they had that. We tried to stay strong but still, our hearts ached.

One morning I was in the basement doing laundry and Tony came down the basement stairs to say goodbye before work. He stopped on the stairs and looked at me. He had black circles under his eyes and he looked gaunt. I felt the pain welling up in my heart and I started to cry. One of the most tragic elements of our infertility that I thought about secretly was that I knew if we had children they would be just like Tony. I couldn't bear the thought that I could not give the world any more Tony's. Tony came down the stairs, and we stood in the basement amongst the dirty laundry piles and cried. It was the lowest moment of the journey. There was nothing to say, no words to make it better, just grief. We let it all out and held each other in silence. Eventually he led me up the stairs into the kitchen.

"Let's pray," he said. We stood in our kitchen and prayed for direction.

Before I had even left for work that morning, our phone rang and it was our Pastor John. He asked me if we had ever considered adoption.

"No, we haven't really talked about it," I said.

"There's a girl in Florida who was pregnant and considering adoption. I don't know if she's sure but I thought you should know." The idea was new and a little scary but smelled of hope.

"I'll certainly talk to Tony John, thank you." I was pretty sure he would like the idea.

I called Tony on his coffee break and told him what Pastor John had said. That evening Tony and I discussed adoption at length. What if she changed her mind? How would we get there? How wonderful it would be! It was a roller coaster of emotion but at the end of it we decided yes, we would like to adopt.

It was only a few days later we learned that she had indeed, changed her mind. At least she did it early, and we weren't too invested. However, the adoption idea was still vital and viable. We met with Pastor John and his wife, Kathie at Bob Evans. They were very encouraging, and we prayed that morning, at that little breakfast table for a family.

The following week I walked into my office at work and found a little newspaper clipping on my desk. It said: If you are interested in adopting a baby from St. Petersburg Russia come to this meeting. Wow, Russia was a long way away. I took the clipping home to Tony, and he suggested we go and learn more.

"It couldn't hurt," he said.

We went to a meeting and met a lawyer and a doctor who partnered together to form an international adoption agency. They were local, and they said they had access to these orphaned babies, so we decided to trust them. We needed to come up with $5,000.00 for a deposit. I had no idea where we could get that money, and we prayed that God would provide. One afternoon my dad called me at work, and he said he had received an unexpected windfall of money, and he and my mum would be honored to pay our down payment. I didn't even know what to say.

"Yes," he said "Just say yes."

"Yes!" I said finally, bursting with excitement and holding back my tears.

The paperwork was unbelievable. Stacks and stacks of forms. Even though we had paid our non-refundable deposit of $5,000.00 we were tasked with getting our own INS approval. We spent months gathering records to verify our identities. There were criminal background checks, medical screenings, fire inspections, verification of banking records, letter from our employers, letter of recommendation, home inspections, adoption classes, parenting classes, a home study by a licensed social worker and the list went on and on. I was glad, however to finally have something constructive to do. It made me feel useful in the prospect of parenthood and I think Tony felt the same way. We had something **to do**. Once we had gathered all of this information and it was organized and copied in triplicate, we sent the package to the INS. We were told it would take 30-90 days and this was before 9-11.

We waited and waited and finally one day we got in our mailbox at home a very special form from the INS called 171-H which said:

NOTICE OF FAVORABLE DETERMINATION CONCERNING APPLICATION FOR ADVANCE PROCESSING OF ORPHAN PETITION.

YOUR ADVANCE PROCESSING APPLICATION HAS BEEN FORWARDED TO THE AMERICAN CONSULATE OR EMBASSY AT MOSCOW RUSSIA, AND CABLE SENT APPROVED FOR ONE (1) CHILD.

Well, there was some dancing going on in our house that night. We were so excited, so full of hope and ready to take this next step.

We called our attorney the following afternoon to find out exactly what our next step would be.

"I'm sorry, Mr. and Mrs. DiTommaso, Russia has issued a moratorium on adoptions at this time," he said flatly.

"What do you mean moratorium?" I was shocked.

"We're sorry, we just don't know any more. There will be no adoptions at this time and we don't know when they will lift the moratorium," his voice trailed off as my hope faded.

"Oh no," I said and looked over at my rabbit. He was visibly growing. I was never sure if Tony could see my rabbit but that afternoon he seemed to be looking right at him too.

Chapter 20

I woke up and looked up at the barn ceiling. The rain was softer but it was still raining quite hard. I looked over at the rabbit. He was still wrapped in the blanket next to me. He opened one eye and smiled.

"Hey," I said. "It's still raining but not as much. We'll stay in here for a little while." He closed his eyes again. I sat up and brushed the hay from my hair and clothes. He sleepily pushed himself up and straightened his legs. Stretching and yawning he shed the blanket from his back and hopped over to me. He looked at me for a long time.

I sighed. "You still want to know if you're the only one. But see, the thing is," I continued, "I'm not entirely sure you are real; I'm not sure you're actually even here." He blinked and twitched his nose.

"Oh, I'm real," he said seriously.

"Well, ok, yes, I suppose I know that you are real." I twisted a thread from my sweatshirt around my skinny finger. "I guess, and please don't be offended but I think you might be dead," he hopped closer to me.

"What's wrong with dead?" he said and smirked.

"Well," I scratched my forehead buying some time, "dead is…well, dead is not good. People don't really talk about the dead and…people certainly shouldn't talk <u>to</u> the dead."

"Why not?" he said without missing a beat and hopping even closer.

"Why not? I repeated loudly. I was getting very uncomfortable.

"Yes, why is dead not good? He tilted his head. "Look, let's just say for a minute I am dead, what is so bad about that?"

I looked at him for a long time. "Because if you were dead, you wouldn't be here with me."

*He looked at me warmly. "You said you weren't sure I **was** here with you."*

"Oh." I had no idea what to say to that. "I'm not really sure about much I guess…but I do know that I like talking to you and being with you. I know that I love you."

He smiled, "I know that. The problem is, I'm not sure though that you do like being with me. See, here's what I know: I know that you would really like to stop carrying me around and you would like to live in a way that you know for certain is real and alive." His back foot suddenly appeared from behind his ear and he leaned back and scratched his head in an amazing way that made me think he had no bones.

"But what would happen to you?" I asked leaning forward and stroking him between the ears.

He smiled. "Nothing would happen to me. I have to leave you soon anyway. Someone will be coming for me," he was speaking softly. "I have a purpose and a place. It's fantastic there. I'll be leaving you, but you will be okay, actually better than okay just as I said."

"I don't want you to go."

"Yes…you do," he winked at me.

"It's fantastic there?" I imagined what it might look like. "How do you know so much about being alive or being dead?" I said finally.

"I know more than you think about life and death. In fact you know what?" he asked with a sparkle in his eye.

"What?" I said picking him up and hugging him.

"I know that you've got a lot of living to do. You've got a very special assignment and it has to do with life. Life is very important and you know what else?" I leaned down closer. "Vi is Latin for life," he whispered in my ear.

"You're certainly the smartest rabbit I know." I set him down poking him playfully and giggling.

We thought for sure the agency would return our deposit. I mean, they hadn't done anything. We had done all the work! We soon came to learn that they were not returning our $5,000.00 and I think we were so shattered at that time that we didn't have the strength to fight for it. We went to see my parents and told them through tears what had happened.

"We can't even return your money," I cried as we sat in their living room.

"The last thing to worry about right now is money. Just take some time to heal and regroup. There's no sense in worrying right now about money," they assured us. The next few weeks were a blur. I felt like a zombie just existing from one moment to the next.

One evening Tony and I were making dinner in silence and he suddenly looked over.

"That couple in our adoption class, they had two babies from Russia. Maybe they can help us." I was not very hopeful but thought it couldn't hurt to call.

"I guess we could try," I said trying to be enthusiastic. Tony had the husband's business card in his wallet and he dialed the number. I was sitting at the dining room table listening to one end of the conversation.

"Uh huh….really….uh huh…yes….well, that's what we suspected… uh huh. Oh really….. Valentine's Day…ok, well…yes…thank you so much….yes, thank you."

"Valentine's Day? What about Valentine's Day?" I whispered.

Tony hung up the phone and looked at me. "There's an international adoption party in Cleveland on Valentine's Day every year." He said half smiling.

"What about the moratorium?" I asked.

"There is no moratorium."

My heart sank. We had lost a year of our lives, and I felt bitterness attempting to plant itself in my heart.

On Valentine's Day 1999 we drove to Cleveland. It was a Sunday and I felt guilty about missing church. As we approached the

Marriott I could see that the parking lot was packed. It was a bright, sunny morning and we walked hand in hand across the crowded parking lot.

Once inside we were asked if we were there for the informational meeting or the party.

"The information I guess," Tony said.

We were escorted to one half of a partitioned ballroom. There were rows of chairs and there were couples seated sporadically in those chairs. We found a place that seemed good enough and sat down. The information meeting was just starting when the speaker asked a series of questions.

"How many of you have had your home study?" Some hands including ours were raised.

"How many of you are in the process of having your home study?" Various hands including ours went up.

"Let's try this, how many of you already have a 171-H INS approval?" she asked, obviously not expecting any hands. Tony and I were the only ones in the group with our hands raised and suddenly felt conspicuous.

"You do?" she asked with great surprise. "Well, we have babies for you. See me after the seminar," she said speaking only to us.

I had trouble listening to any more of the information she was providing because all I could hear in my head was "We have babies for you…" It seemed to take forever, and there was a question and answer period which went on and on. Finally, the speaker drew the meeting to a close and directed our attention to the ballroom partition. Suddenly, I could hear Neil Diamond's "We Come to America" and the partition opened. As far as I could see there were families all having a great big party and there were children of all ages running around. Some families had little babies; some families had toddlers, just every range of ages imaginable.

"These are all our international adoption families!" she said presenting them proudly.

I felt a wave of emotion which was almost uncontrollable and I began to cry, but it was happy cry. It was the kind of cry that makes you embarrassed that you are so sappy. My eyes went from family to family just taking it all in. It was an amazing moment with hope staring us in the face and Neil Diamond didn't hurt either.

As we were milling around the ballroom the speaker found us and we introduced ourselves. She said she was excited to meet us, and that if we had our 171-H, we were all ready to go. She directed our attention to some flyers on a table.

"These are all available children." she said. There must have been 12 babies on that flyer.

"I would like to schedule you to come to our office one evening this week and I will show you some videos," she continued.

We were nervous and it felt like a whirlwind, but we agreed.

On February 18, we drove to the offices of the adoption agency. We were greeted by what looked like Santa's workshop. There were dozens of people working and filing and typing, answering phones and meeting with hopeful looking couples.

"Come on through," the woman who came to be known as Margaret said as she led us through the agency into a small room. There she produced a few videotapes.

"We have a very special baby picked just for you," she said popping the VHS into the tape deck. Tony held my hand as we saw the image of a little baby on the screen.

"Oh sorry, that's the wrong one," she said moving toward the television.

"No leave it," Tony said gently touching her arm. She smiled.

"This one is….Vitaly," she said reading off the tape box.

"Vitaly," we both said watching him bounce his hips up and down. He had the prettiest eyes I had ever seen.

"That sounds Italian." Tony gave me a big grin.

"So, we would like for you to watch a few…," she said as she popped the tape. She showed us a few videos.

"We'd like to see that Vitaly again," Tony said as he smiled at me.

"Sure thing," she said happily putting the tape back in.

"Still, we would like you to take two videos home with you and watch them both. Who would you like?" she asked.

"Definitely Vitaly" Tony said, "…and Alexander?" he continued looking at me for guidance.

"Yes fine. Vitaly for sure and Alexander too," I said. This was quite surreal.

"Vitaly is a very common Russian name which means life," she said smiling and my heart leapt.

We were given a package of information that would guide us through the steps we were about to take, hugged, and sent home with our videos. When we got home that night we briefly looked at the paperwork and gasped at the money we would have to find, but soon settled in to watch the videos over and over… and over and over.

"How do we possibly pick?" I asked Tony as we were watching the screen.

"We are just going to have to pray and pray some more," he said without taking his eyes off Vitaly.

We agreed to pray for the next 24 hours and then after that time we would tell each other what God had said. The whole next day we prayed and prayed. I had an appointment that evening to get my hair done, and I prayed through my highlight session. I was driving out of downtown Sharon, Pennsylvania when my cell phone rang.

"I know which baby," Tony said.

My words were stuck in my throat. "Me too," I said nervously. It hadn't been 24 hours but I knew, more than I had ever known anything before, which baby was our son. There was a long silence, and we both knew the significance of what was about to happen. *What if we didn't agree?* It was a scary moment and time seemed to stand still.

"I want you to go first," I said.

"Ok… I can't wait any longer. For me it's Vitaly," he said.

"ME TOO!" I screamed into the phone. There was laughing and crying on the other end of the phone.

"Where are you? Come home!" He blurted excitedly.

I pulled into the driveway and ran into the house. We embraced and cried happy tears. But w*hat now?* We were both thinking.

Vitaly was born in February. We had learned that he was our son on the day before his first birthday. It took every ounce of self-control we had between us, but we decided to wait until the next day to tell our families. We went to our local baker and asked them to make three little birthday cakes, each with the words "Happy Birthday, Vitaly."

One by one we went to our parents' homes and gave them each a cake.

They looked confused, obliged, and said "Ok, so who is Vitaly?"

"He's your grandson and he's one today!" we declared.

They each had very satisfying reactions: tears, hugs, praises to God. Tony's father's reaction sticks in my mind. He just sat down and stared at the table. It was shock, good shock. He is himself an immigrant and came to the United States all alone as a young boy, and I think in that moment he related to his brand new grandson in a way none of us could match.

It was a glorious afternoon especially when we realized that Vitaly had been born the day of or very close to the day our in-vitro stopped. We knew God was in control, but the sobering reality was we still had to get to Russia, we still had to come up with tens of thousands of dollars, and we had an empty yellow room for a nursery. The next morning we were told we had a March court date in Moscow. It was an absolute flurry of activity.

My wonderful friends and family planned, in those few short days, the biggest, most amazing baby shower anyone could ask for. They had wonderful favors and beautiful invitations and I was completely overwhelmed. One of the favors was a candle each for everyone to light and pray for us while we were in Russia. As if I needed another reason to be emotional! That night following the baby shower we went to our local watering hole and perfect strangers were coming up to us and handing us money. Our families had already come together and given us money, and Tony's brother and his wife had bought us a brand new video camera. They told us that it was important to document everything for later years. We were speechless.

We had a phone call from Margaret at ECC who said that the orphanage had a German measles scare and that they had to delay our court date. It was nerve racking but she assured us it was only a slight delay and right then and there she gave us our new court date, March 24. The money came. I don't really know all the sources but it just came and we booked our flights.

We had a list of items we had to bring with us, amazing things like perfume and a certain brand of coffee, a gold chain and various other items. We were not naïve and went in with both eyes open.   The night before we left we inventoried our gifts, packed our bags, and both of us sat on the floor of our new nursery. It was now overflowing with baby supplies all ready for Vitaly's arrival in 10 days.   I hovered over all the paperwork which we had accumulated over the months of preparation. I had 3- hole punch binders, 3 of them. There was one to pack in each of our suitcases in case one was lost and one for my carry-on bag. The one in my carry-on bag had all the original documents and seals. There wasn't much room in my carry-on bag because I had my rabbit in there, but I had enough room for everything I thought I needed. We were as ready as anyone has ever been for our new adventure as parents.

Chapter 21

"So who is coming to get you?" I asked pulling my coat around myself and shivering. Winter had definitively arrived on Old Orchard Hill. I could see my breath as I spoke and two sets of footsteps in the snow followed us, my boot prints and his paw prints. The rabbit was obviously cold, and I picked him up and zipped him inside my coat. His fur was soft and warm.

"Someone you know very well," he whispered. Unexpectedly, my grandfather's face popped into my head.

"Granddad?" I said perplexed. He smiled in a way that made me feel very naive.

"No, not Granddad," small puffs of steam came from his little rabbit mouth as he spoke.

I thought for a long time. "Is it God?" A big wave of excitement came over me. He smiled knowingly and snuggled into my neck.

"Brrrr, it's cold out here," he said changing the subject. "Don't you think we should find shelter?"

"If it is God, you have to tell me. I would let you go with God," I said eagerly as if this was new information.

The rabbit shivered. "Look, you and I standing out in the freezing cold is not doing anybody any good," he said. I looked around at the barren landscape. The trees were bare and everything was covered in white. I wanted to keep talking.

"The barn?" I said hopefully

"Ok, the barn then," he stuttered as he spoke.

Once inside the warmth of the barn I plopped down on a bale of hay. I heard a few creatures who had sought shelter in the barn scurry out upon our arrival.

I unzipped my coat and the rabbit sat quietly looking at me on my lap.

"So, is it God?" I insisted. He looked at me and his eyes were so warm and gentle.

"His name is Jesus," he blinked slowly and I felt heat spread like waves from my heart over my entire body.

"Jesus?" I said quietly. "Yes, you were right, I do know Him."

"He's coming to take me from you…if you will let me go," he said gently.

Tears streamed down my face as I thought about letting him go.

"So then, he'll carry you?" I asked hopefully.

"He's been carrying us both for a long time."

I let out a long overdue exhale, then I hung my head. "What if I'm not ready yet?"

"You will be when the time comes." He snuggled into me and I was happy just to hold him a little while longer.

The next morning Tony's mother and stepfather arrived to drive us to the airport. It was a beautiful sunshiny day. I stared out the window at the horizon and thought it was all too good to be true. I kept thinking I would wake up and realize it had all been a dream. The flight to Moscow was very long, but it was also very exciting. I had no idea what to expect on the other side. Tony and I had made many trips to England and Wales and various places in the United States, but Russia was another story entirely.   We noticed that another couple on the plane was carrying an ECC bag.

"Go ask!" I said as I gently pushed on Tony's arm.

"I'll go to the bathroom," he said unbuckling his seatbelt. He was gone a few minutes and suddenly plopped back down in his seat.

"Yes, they're from Michigan and they're adopting too. They'll be with us." A wave of relief came over me, and we became fast friends on that plane.

Upon arrival at the Moscow airport we were greeted by the Russian Customs Officers. I felt like I was in a movie. It was pretty scary… rather, they were pretty scary. They had big fur hats just like in the movies which I came to learn were called Ushankas. They were clearly not open and friendly people. I stayed very close to Tony, and we made our way through with a series of nods and grunts. On the other side of customs were lines of people holding signs. We saw a sign with our name on it and introduced ourselves to Serge and Demitri, our driver and our interpreter. We were escorted into a van with Sam and Kim, the couple from the plane, and several other American couples. We were relieved of our "gifts" which were loaded into the back of the van. Before Serge even moved, Demitri turned around and said in a very thick Russian voice, "Who is DiTommaso?" We waved to identify ourselves.

"Your baby is sick, in the hospital and may or may not be able to travel." Then he turned back around in his seat and Serge started the van. I looked over at Tony who gave me a comforting sort of smile. "It will be ok," he said. I tried to relax but that was not what I had expected to hear.

We were driven to the Hotel Ukraine which is a magnificent hotel in the center of Moscow. It is absolutely breathtaking. The lobby was more like a giant marble ballroom with beautiful antique sofas and wonderful giant rugs. As we walked in the lobby, I became aware of men stationed around the place with big guns and big walkie talkies. We also noticed little groups of people gathered around televisions in the massive lobby watching the news. Demitri walked over to the crowd and we could overhear a conversation all in Russian.

"What's going on?" Tony sidled over and leaned toward Demitri.

"America began airstrikes on Kosovo this afternoon so you should be *discreet* about being

American." *Discreet?* We could blend in only so much with all the black clothes. Tony made his way back to me.

"We'll be ok, Suz, we'll keep our mouths shut and our eyes and ears open." He squeezed my hand. We were instructed to check all of our money at the guest desk, exchange a small amount, and get settled into our rooms. Demitri said we would be given our itinerary the next day.

Tony and I found our room which was somewhat cold but still quite beautiful. The walls were light blue and there was a magnificent red rug in between the two twin beds with gold bedding and gold braiding. I sat on the bed and stared at the beautifully crafted rug. I just couldn't believe I was sitting in a hotel in Moscow, Russia. Tony sat on the bed next to me and bounced up and down wiggling his eyebrows.

"Stop that," I said playfully.

"Sam said they had a pizza delivery place. What do you think?" he asked showing me a take- out menu.

"You think it will be any good?" I took the menu from him.

"Rumor is that it's *American style*," he replied with a chuckle.

"Let's do it." I was hungry and pizza sounded good. Tony dialed the phone and I heard him ordering a cheese pizza. It seemed surreal to me to sit in Moscow eating pizza the night before we were going to meet our son.

Tony was still on the phone when I got up and walked to the big window. I separated the huge drapes and looked out into the cold, snowy Moscow night. A man in a Ushanka was walking across the courtyard. I stared at him and wondered how incredibly different his life must be from mine. Just then Tony slid in next to me between the drapes.

"Incredible isn't it?" he said looking at the scenery and slipping his hand around my waist. I nodded and just then I noticed something in the snow. It was snowing quite hard at this point but it was unmistakable. It was my lion. He walked very slowly across the courtyard seemingly unaffected by the cold wind. I watched him disappear into the night. I looked over and Tony was watching him too. He smiled. We were so glad He was there with us.

The next morning Demitri knocked on our door.

"Today we go to government offices and get many stamps and seals required for the adoption. Be in lobby in 20 minutes," he said with authority.

"Will we see our baby today?" I piped up. He looked at his clipboard. "DiTommaso…your baby is in hospital. We will see about getting permission to see him." My heart felt shaky in my chest. I hugged my rabbit.

"What's wrong with him?" I asked. He looked at me as if I were hard of hearing.

"He is in hospital," he said matter of factly and walked out the door.

We met in the lobby of the Hotel Ukraine. Sam and Kim were there along with another couple from Illinois. We all piled into the van. There was some idle chatter about the weather and the flights but not much conversation about where we were going and what we were doing. Again, we kept our mouths shut. Serge drove us all around Moscow that morning. We would pull up in front of a building, Demitri would ask for one of our many forms, he would retrieve a gift or two from the back of the van and then disappear into a side door. Thirty minutes or so later he would reappear with various stamps, seals, and signatures. The forms were all in Russian, and we had no idea what purpose they served. We knew only that these official stamps and whatnots were helping us get to Vitaly. This was our only activity the first day.

That evening there was a knock on our hotel room door. Demetri entered looking officious.

"Your son is still in hospital. Tomorrow we take other families to orphanage and take you to hospital to see your child. Is four hours north. Yes?" he said.

"Yes. Thank you," we said willingly.

The next morning we made the long ride north. Serge wasted no time as we raced up the Russian countryside. There were no seat belts in the van. It seemed to take forever but eventually we arrived at a hotel. It was a big brand new hotel seemingly appearing out of nowhere. We had only brought enough things for a few days and Demetri carried our smaller luggage to our room. "Today?" I said to him as he was leaving. "Today," he said nodding officiously yet warmly.

A few hours later Demetri knocked on the door.

"We go to hospital," he said. I stood up nervously. I looked at my rabbit in my arms. He was heavy that day and I wanted to put him on the bed and leave him there. I just couldn't make myself set him down. Demetri was waiting and staring at me so I carried him out to the van.   Serge drove us to a building in a small town. Demitri got out of the van and entered the building.

"Is this the hospital?" Tony asked. Serge's English was not very good, but we made out that we were picking up a social worker. A woman in a big fur coat and fur hat nodded to us as she climbed into the van. We attempted to speak to her but she clearly spoke no English. It was another 30 minute drive until we pulled up in front of a run-down tan building. It seemed to have no glass in the windows. This couldn't be the hospital. It was very cold that day and the snow was very deep. Demetri opened the van door and put his hand out for me.

"This is hospital," he said helping me out of the van. My heart was racing and I thought I might faint. We were about to meet our son. We followed Demetri and the woman in the fur coat across the courtyard and into the entrance of the hospital. The halls made big echoes as we walked through. We were led down many corridors. It was like a big maze of halls with room after room. As we passed we could see patients in their beds. One particular room had a little girl with a bare light bulb. Her mother looked up and right at me over the handkerchief tied on her face.

Eventually we stopped at a door with a large padlock. A nurse arrived with a key. *Was he locked in there?* I thought. She unlocked the door and motioned for us to enter.

"In," she said flatly. There was light green vinyl siding on the walls and wooden benches around the perimeter with a small table in the corner. It was a cold room with no windows. Demetri, the woman in the fur coat and the nurse turned around and walked out. We heard the door lock behind them. Tony and I stared at each other.

"Now what?" I whispered. I was scared, very scared. It was then that I saw him. I didn't even wonder how he had gotten into that room.

His massive frame swirled the air around us. He walked very slowly and stopped and stood next to me. He didn't look right at me but he put his face very close to my rabbit. I could hear him breathing and I could feel the warmth coming from his fur. He lowered his massive head and nudged my rabbit. I pulled my rabbit close. I heard a very low growl and the Lion kept walking. He got to the corner of the room and began to circle and circle as if he was going to lie down. He stopped and looked at me again before flopping down on the floor. His enormous body took up one whole side of that room and his tail swished gently. Finally, he lowered his head and I heard and felt his exhale. I was so glad he was there.

Tony and I sat very close to each other on the bench and he held my hand. "Ready?" he asked me. I could only nod. Tony began to pray. The minutes dragged on until finally we heard a key in the door. The threesome entered the room only this time the nurse was carrying a huge bundle of white. I couldn't breathe. She placed the bundle on the table in the corner and began to unwrap. It was like a Christmas present that was wrapped in many layers of papers. Her back was to us and our view was obstructed until finally she turned around and produced a little baby boy. His hair was long and curly and he was wearing green pants and pink socks. He had a binky in his mouth and she handed him to Tony.

"Hey there little guy," Tony whispered as he pulled him close and held him gently. Vitaly seemed a little scared as if he had just been woken up.   He was quite wriggly and squirmed in Tony's arms. Tony looked at me and motioned for me to take the baby. I dropped my rabbit which landed with a thud and Tony's eyes looked stern. I reached for him and took him in my arms. He was very slight. His body was just so very light and his limbs were so small and he seemed unable to hold up his head. Just as I was staring into his beautiful blue eyes he reached for my glasses.

"Hey," I laughed as he pulled them off and began to inspect them. Demetri was taking pictures and Tony handed him our video camera. It was all so overwhelming. The woman in the fur coat stood in the corner and several other nurses had now entered the room. Every time another person would enter the room my Lion would lift His head protectively. I couldn't believe that I was holding my son in my arms. He was so very light and he felt like a dream. Suddenly the nurse came and reached for him.

"Already?" I said with slight panic. Demetri nodded for me to give her back the baby. Tony and I both kissed him on the head and reluctantly handed him back.

"How long?" Tony had pulled Demetri aside and was whispering. Demetri shrugged and said something we could not understand. The nurse bundled Vitaly up quickly, took him out and we were escorted out of the room. I could see the nurse in the hall up ahead and just the top of the white bundle. I became very dizzy and disorientated as she disappeared around the corner. My rabbit was so big that day that I struggled to carry him.

As we got out into the courtyard I felt my knees giving out and could feel Tony's strong arm lifting up my body to keep me going.

"Will we see him again?" I aske and I could feel the tears coming.

"Keep walking, just keep walking," he said quietly. Just then I dropped my rabbit in the snow and collapsed. Tony was reaching for me, trying to gather me up, when I saw my Lion come from behind him. Tony moved aside as the Lion slowly moved closer. He gently nudged my rabbit lying limp in the snow.

"She needs you," Tony said and he put my arm up on the Lion and gently lifted me onto his huge neck. I felt the warmth of his body as I held onto his mane. The Lion gently picked up my rabbit and carried it as I rode on his back through the deep snow of the courtyard. Tony walked alongside, close to the Lion's head. When we got to the van the Lion lowered himself so that Tony could help me inside. I retrieved my rabbit and saw my husband give the Lion a quick and grateful hug.

    We arrived back at the hotel and the other families were all in the lobby excitedly discussing their trip to the orphanage. They showed us pictures of their babies, and they all seemed to have a plan. *What was our plan? Were we going to be able to take Vitaly home?* I tried to be pleasant briefly, but excused myself to go the hotel room. Tony followed me and once in the safety of our room I allowed myself to cry.

    I must have fallen asleep on the bed because when I woke up it was evening. Tony was sitting in front of the television watching the news with the sound very low. "What's going on?" I asked trying to focus my eyes.

    "Oh, nothing everything is ok," he said turning off the television, but he looked a little worried and I knew our country was at war.

    "You ok?" he said. I just sat in silence.

    "I don't know," I said.

    "Let's watch the video," he said encouragingly. We didn't have much footage but I just had to see Vitaly again so we curled up together and watched the tiny screen. My heart ached as I imagined him somewhere without us at that very moment.

    Just then Demetri knocked on our door. He looked at me, and then asked to have a quiet word with Tony. They moved out into the hall and I could hear Tony asking Demetri to find out why Vitaly was in the hospital, and if he was going to be ok.

"Thank you…thank you Demetri," I heard Tony say quietly as he closed the door. I heard something brush on the door and then a massive thud. Neither one of us moved. We both knew it was our Lion guarding our door.

"We need to pray," Tony said. I knew that he was definitely right and we both got on our knees and began to pray. We must have prayed and read scripture all night long. It was the longest night of my life. I had to reach very deep to gather up every ounce of faith and trust I had ever had. I had never been so pressed and tested. As the sun rose that morning I began to have a new song in my heart. The seeds of hope had sprouted, and I knew that no matter what happened we would take our son home. We had decided that if we had to live in Russia until he was well enough to travel that's what we would do. The "no matter what" plan was in place.

We were dressed and ready for whatever God had in store for us that day when Demetri knocked on our door once again. He came right into the room and this time the sun was shining brightly through the window. He explained to us that Vitaly had an ear infection and was doing much better. He was quite certain that once they had completed the medication course he would be ready to go home with us.

"One, maybe two days," he said. I felt a flood of relief and wanted to hug him. *He must have been up all night*, I thought to myself.

That day Tony and I walked all around that little town and took lots of video. It was cold but very sunny. The other couples had gone back to the orphanage to get their babies but I had such peace in my heart that I didn't mind that we had to wait a little while longer. We strolled the streets arm in arm, video camera in hand. Trolley cars on cables clamored noisily by us full of bundled up Russian people. We saw a milk truck in what looked like a park with a long line of people waiting with jugs. We turned down one small alley and there were cars buried up to their roofs in snow. People shuffled by wearing big coats and scurried down little cellar doors of dark brown wooden row houses. Almost everyone smoked, and the people were just so strikingly beautiful. We videotaped it all for Vitaly to see one day when he was older.

Late that afternoon we had a much unexpected surprise. Demetri arrived and whisked us off into the van.

"We have to get passport photo and you can see your son," he said. We got the sense that this was not business as usual and sat in silence gratefully. We stopped at the same building in town and retrieved the fur coat clad social worker. She was much less scary this time and smiled to me when she climbed in. We entered the hospital grounds and the social worker motioned for us to stay in the van. We complied and she and Demetri disappeared through the hospital entrance. It seemed to take forever as we sat in the van listening to Serge's pop music quietly play on the radio. Finally, we saw the silhouette of a woman carrying a bundle.

"Here he comes," Tony said squeezing my hand.

We saw Vitaly for just a few moments that day. I got to hold him while he had his photo taken and he was very chipper. He was obviously feeling much better. We kissed him goodbye, told him we would see him in a day or so, and gave him back to Demetri. We went to bed early that night because we had a very special court date the next day.

Chapter 22

It was finally the day we had been waiting for, our adoption day in court. I was up very early and put on my best dress I had brought for this very occasion. Tony was done up in his best suit and we were driven to the courthouse. It was a huge stone building with very cold architecture, somewhat like I imagined a big Russian prison. We were dropped in the front of the building on the sidewalk, and we followed Demetri out of the cold street air into the musty but warm government building. The hallway was eerie and our footsteps echoed. We could hear distant typewriters and phones ringing. Official business was in full swing. The high ceilings had evidence of leaking and the paint was peeling on the walls. I was not expecting the courthouse to be such an unpleasant place. We were escorted down a long corridor with many open doors and benches all down each side.

We followed Demetri up a curving stairwell which echoed even more than the hallway and through a creaky door at the top which slammed when it closed. We walked down the second floor hallway.

"This is Attorney Edgar. He will be your attorney,"Demitri announced. A man in a suit with dark hair thrust his hand out to Tony. I had no idea we would need an attorney and I began to get nervous again.

"I am your attorney. In hearing there will be prosecutor in the courtroom. He will try to stop adoption - - I will do my best to convince the judge to let us take Vitaly to America." My pulse quickened and I could hear my heartbeat in my ears. I felt dizzy.

"I have good track record with judge, and I think everything will work out fine." He then brought us in close. "We volunteer nothing about a hospital. If the judge finds out about the hospital she may not approve your application. Let's hope she doesn't ask." Edgar gave us a stern look and motioned for us to be seated until our names were called. Tony and I sat on the bench.

"Oh God honey. What are we going to do? We can't lie," I whispered.

"God will protect us," he told me. "Let's pray."

We prayed that the judge would not ask anything about the hospital. As the fear and dread began to spread throughout my body I fought back by singing praise songs as loud as I could in my head to drown out all else and calmly stroked my rabbit.

Finally, our names were called. I shoved my rabbit way down in my bag and zipped him up in it so that no one would see him or suspect even a hint of his presence. Then, we were escorted into the courtroom. The courtroom was smaller than I had expected and quite crowded. I wasn't sure who all the people were, but they all sat in silence on cold metal chairs and glared at us. Although we had an interpreter, I could not understand any of the proceedings.

We were seated at a big, wooden table in front of the judge, and a man with a purple tie said some apparently derogatory things about us. Attorney Edgar would stand up and fight on our behalf. The judge seemed to be looking at something while she listened. She asked us to speak and explain why we would be good parents to this child which we did. She stared at us as the interpreter conveyed our words. I was very uneasy about the interpretation as the room seemed ever so adversarial and I had no idea what was actually being said. The judge listened and looked at our file. She asked nothing of Vitaly's whereabouts.

There was a long silence and no one moved. Finally, she made a bold announcement in Russian. I was only aware of the voice of the interpreter who said, "You have obviously bonded with this baby. Orphan Petition for Adoption approved immediately, mandatory 10 day waiting period is waived. You are free to obtain Visa and leave the country with this child." Then I heard the gavel bang.

I looked over at Demetri and his eyes were smiling although he was not. Inside I was jumping up and down but I remained cool and poised. Demetri approached the bench, said something politely in Russian to the judge and she handed him our file. I caught her eye and I sensed the slightest hint of warmth. She looked away quickly and got down from the bench. Demetri escorted us out into the hall and showed us that the Judge had been looking at the pictures he had taken of our first encounter with Vitaly. I stared at the picture of me embracing my son, both of us with our eyes closed like we had known each other forever.

Tony and I hugged and I could feel the excitement and his heart beating in his chest. We saw Sam and Kim coming down the hall from a different courtroom grinning from ear to ear.

"Are you approved?" we asked excitedly of each other. "Yes!" we all cried out in unison jumping and hugging each other in the corridor. We made our way out to the van where Serge was waiting with a big grin.

"Ok?" he said supportively nodding.

"Yep, everything is ok," I said as I climbed in. He said the same to each couple as they climbed in. What a wonderful driver he was.

We updated our families that night via telephone. All the couples then had a celebratory 6 or 7 course dinner in the hotel. We had been through a lot together and it was a wonderful evening. Little did we know what was yet to come.

The next day we were instructed to pack all of our belongings as we were returning to Moscow. Serge arrived to take Tony and I to the hospital to get Vitaly once and for all. This would be the day that we would become a family for good. We stopped to get our social worker and arrived at the hospital. We were escorted into the same pad locked room. It didn't seem quite so cold that day.

A nurse came in carrying a bundle and unwrapped him on the same corner table. There he was, our son. As I stood admiring him I noticed the nurse was crying as she removed his clothing. Another nurse came in and pushed the crying nurse out of the room. Tony moved forward to pick up Vitaly, but a nurse put her hand out to stop him.

"Mother?" she pointed to me and motioned for me to dress the baby.

Tony had taught me in the hotel room how to diaper and dress a bed pillow because he had three younger brothers. I had very little experience with babies and Vitaly wriggled much more than the hotel bed pillow. I felt all eyes on me as I began to dress him. Tony stood close by and I could feel him cheering me on. I got the shirt on, the binky in and the socks on. I looked at Tony holding the diaper bag.

"Pants....pants....where were the pants?" I whispered. I could see the bottom of the diaper bag and there were no pants in sight. Tony smiled at me and I could read his eyes telling me to fake it. I confidently pulled his socks all the way up his legs and zipped him into his light blue reindeer snuggly from Auntie Beth. I gathered him up in my arms and smelled him. I was a mother, and I had never felt that depth of love before in my whole life. I turned to the nurses.

"Thank you," I said really trying not to burst into tears.

Just then I realized how hard it must be for those nurses to say goodbye. I suddenly knew how much love they had poured into Vitaly in the first year of his life. I tried smiling although I had tears coming, and Demetri led our new little family out into the hall. I saw the young nurse who had brought him in standing in the hall, still crying. I walked up to her and she looked down and backed away.

"We will take good care of him," I said softly. She looked up for a brief second and I saw her big blue eyes wet with tears. I don't know if she understood, but she smiled at me with her eyes before she was shooed away by an obviously senior staff nurse.

"Can you ask them what he likes to eat?" Tony said to Demetri who in turn spoke in Russian to the nurses as he corralled us down the corridor.

"Buckwheat yogurt," he replied.

Chapter 23

The ride back to Moscow was pretty long with the babies in the van and not a car seat or seatbelt to be found. I was perfectly happy to hold Vitaly but he was not very happy about being held for that long. We took turns holding him all the way. He had barely made any sound in our presence with the exception of his horrendous deep cough, but at one point in the journey he let out such a long wail that seemed to go on forever and we were absolutely impressed.

"He's got good lungs!" Tony said smiling.

By the time we arrived at the hotel Ukraine, Vitaly really wanted to be put down. Tony carried him into the lobby and laid him out on the nearest couch. He seemed much happier then but looked very sleepy and rocked his head. We gave him a few minutes of couch time before we carried him up to our room. The sun was setting and as the Moscow night fell, we tucked Vitaly all snuggly with blankets in a suitcase on the floor. We both stretched out on the floor on either side of this suitcase and watched him sleep. He was snoring ever so slightly and we had full hearts. It was our first night as a family. I had no idea where my rabbit was, nor did I care. I knew as always, he would turn up again eventually.

The next morning we had the opportunity to go on a tour of the various sights of Moscow. When our tour guide and bus arrived, Tony asked the pretty tour guide, "How long is the trip? Should we should bring a stroller?"

"No stroller, we walk," Nadia answered. We were paying her by the hour and soon learned just how long a tour of Moscow can be. It was bright and sunny but was still a very cold Moscow morning. Vitaly was coughing a lot that day but we kept him completely bundled up. He slept almost the whole time. We saw St. Basil's cathedral, Red Square, and loads of churches with fantastic architecture. It was all very beautiful but a few hours into the tour, as much as we loved carrying him, we couldn't take it anymore. Tony tapped Nadia on the shoulder.

"We have to go back," he said. She was not easily convinced.

"No, no, there is more," she said and shook her head.

"No, that is enough. We are finished." Tony had to quite firm with her. I was so glad. Vitaly and I were both ready to go back. Climbing into the van I laid Vitaly on the seat next to me. I wished I had a car seat for him. He fell right back to asleep, and the only sound he made was a frequent deep cough.

We finally arrived back at our hotel room and rested our tired legs and arms. As night fell on our second night as a family, there was a knock on the hotel room door. It was Demetri. He came in and closed the door. His voice was soft as he spoke to us.

"Listen to me, the conflict with Kosovo has escalated. We don't want to take any chances and we are advising everyone to stay in hotel rooms as much as possible. So, you stay inside, da?"

"Da," we said in unison, which means yes.

"I go to tell the others," he turned to leave.

"Wait, Demetri," Tony said. "We need to find something for Vitaly to eat." I was getting worried now. Vitaly had eaten precious little since we got him. We tried some baby food but he did not seem interested. He did not seem to understand the bottle and we had been dropping water in his mouth with an eye dropper we got at the adoption center headquarters.

"There is shop around the corner. He eats yogurt." He looked Tony squarely in the eye. "Be careful and be discreet."

"Da. Spasiba." Tony said "yes" and "thank you" and nodded militantly. Demetri left our room. Tony walked behind him and locked the deadbolt.

"We are ok." He said looking at me. I was holding Vitaly in one arm and my rabbit in the other. That night we watched CNBC and tried to understand what, if any danger, we were in.

The next morning Tony left and went to the shop around the corner as instructed and bought some yogurt. We managed to get a little bit in him, but Vitaly was not very interested in food. He was very sleepy. We had been dosing him with Tylenol and his antibiotic from the hospital and knew that given the bronchitis in his chest, sleep was the best thing for him. That day we stayed in our hotel and watched him sleep. Tony would leave periodically to get supplies, mainly because he can't sit still that long. Myself, I was perfectly content to stay in the safety of the dead bolted room with my brand new son.

Periodically, Tony would convince me to walk the halls with Vitaly in his stroller, and we walked for what seemed to be miles of beautifully crafted, perfectly polished, herringbone wooden hallways. Vitaly seemed to really enjoy the movement and his eyes were wide with wonder of all he could see as he sat up in that umbrella stroller.

In the evenings we called our families one by one and they felt a world away.

"Please pray for him. He's very little."

"Come home safely," the voices said on the end of the phone, distant and distracted.

I asked my sister-in-law's advice on the Tylenol because they have three kids. Everyone sounded somewhat bewildered. I attributed it to the war and the telephone connection.

Sometime in the afternoon Demetri came by. We had an appointment the next morning with our Embassy to get Vitaly's Visa so that we could get him home.

Demetri closed the door and spoke very sternly again. "Terrorists have attacked the American Embassy with grenade launchers and the riot police shot them dead in the street. We will be unable to go to the main embassy area." He stood very still. "We will bring you in the backdoor disguised as American Embassy workers."

"American Embassy workers with babies?" My voice shook as I spoke. Demetri ignored my question. He turned to leave but just as he did he turned back.

"There is some kind of problem with your paperwork. We go before sunrise." He started back for the door. "Be in lobby at 5:00 a.m."

Chapter 24

The wind howled outside the barn and every so often a big gust of cold air would burst under the barn door. We were warm and sheltered in our little barn, the rabbit and I.

"It sounds pretty awful out there." I said listening to the bitter cold wind and the branches beating against the siding. "We might be stuck in here for a while."

"It will pass," the rabbit said but he seemed distracted and he paused and looked deep into my eyes. "I think we should try something." I didn't like his tone of voice.

"Like what?" I said suspiciously.

"Like… you should go on without me and…."

"No… I," I interrupted him then stopped. "Go on where anyway?"

"Just listen," he continued. "You should go on and I will stay right here. You come back and I'll still be here. Like a trial run."

"Right in the middle of a winter snow storm?" I said desperately.

"I'm safe and warm, look," he said curling up in a little bed of hay we had created earlier and smiling mischievously.

I looked at his little gray face. "I don't want to." I stroked his soft side as he lay.

"I know," he said sighing. "I understand, but I'm not meant to stay with you."

"You're not?" I said but I already knew that.

"No, I'm not. You've got an important assignment and I will just hold you back."

"No you won't!" I insisted. "Plus, what about foxes and…"

"I told you I don't worry about foxes and badgers. Truth is I won't sleep here."

"But you said you would stay here!" I did not like this deal at all.

He smiled, "You don't understand, but that's ok, you aren't supposed to understand."

I thought deeply. "Jesus?"

"Yes, Jesus."

*"But, you'll be here if I come back for you? I mean **when** I come back for you."*

*"Yep. I will be here until **you** hand me over" and he hopped towards me.*

"Let me think about it," I said lifting him to my lap.

He sighed and leaned in to me.

We didn't sleep much that night. Tony watched the news and I walked back and forth rocking Vitaly. He had come to like being rocked but quite hard, more like a swinging motion. The kind of movement that is good for the waistline. We didn't talk much about what we might encounter at the Embassy. Sometime around 4:00 a.m. Tony suggested we pray. We asked God to cover us and our new friends as we took this final step to get our babies home.

We asked God to open doors that might be closed and to deliver us safely.

We met Demetri as instructed in the lobby. We all piled into the van in silence and drove through the predawn Moscow Streets. Upon arriving at the Embassy we were hurried out of the van and pushed toward the back door.

"Run," Demetri whispered making a motion for us to run and we complied. There were lines of soldiers and riot police in the street and it was impossible to determine their nationality in the dark. There were also many shadowy figures moving about in the city and around the back door of the embassy. Also many giant statues were all around the courtyard and it was hard to determine which shadows were being made by people and which shadows were being made my statues. Just then I saw a familiar shadow, a shadow that had no ominous accompaniment. The Lion of Judah walked before us as we entered the back door. He was enormous and his paws shook the earth as he led the way.

We followed the Lion inside and once we were inside we felt a little bit of relief. We were taken into a cafeteria where they had tables set up as makeshift offices.

"This is where the Embassy workers had been moved to the basement for their safety," Demetri said calmly. This was normally where the American Embassy workers recreated.

There was a snack counter and what looked like a bar/pool hall on the perimeter. The room was tense and on edge.

"Sit and be silent." He motioned to some cold blue plastic chairs. "They are getting people processed as fast as they can." We sat in cold plastic chairs and watched Vitaly sleep. He was in his reindeer snuggly from Auntie Beth and oblivious to anything going on around him. Our Lion was on the floor nearby and had my rabbit in his custody. It seemed ages and we suddenly heard a stern voice.

"DiTommaso?" Tony motioned for me to stay seated and he walked toward the embassy agent.

"You sir, do not have an appointment!" he shouted at Tony pointing into his chest. Tony began to speak but was interrupted.

"You sir, and your family have placed everyone in this room in danger!" He was very rude and I could see Tony starting to lose his temper. Our Lion had moved and was now standing behind Tony. I saw him gently drop my rabbit on the floor and then lift his head protectively.

"Your 171-H has not been received and you cannot get an appointment for a Visa for your son without it," the agent continued very rudely. The Lion began a slow roar which slowly grew and grew until it was deafening and as the agent stared at the lion all the color ran from his face. Tony looked squarely at the young man and backed away slowly.

"You wait right there," he said gritting his teeth. He was coming toward me now and he looked very, very angry. My husband is one of the physically strongest people I had ever met, but he was always under control. I did not want to see that change that day. Our Lion kept the agent in his place while Tony spoke to me. "Give me the original 171-H and pray," he whispered in my ear with one eye on the agent. I reached in my backpack and pulled out my three ring binder. Page one was our original, signed171-H with a raised seal which you may remember read:

NOTICE OF FAVORABLE DETERMINATION CONCERNING APPLICATION FOR ADVANCE PROCESSING OF ORPHAN PETITION.

YOUR ADVANCE PROCESSING APPLICATION HAS BEEN FORWARDED TO THE AMERICAN CONSULATE OR EMBASSY AT MOSCOW RUSSIA, AND CABLE SENT APPROVED FOR ONE (1) CHILD.

I handed the form to Tony. He walked back to the agent and handed him the form. His voice was low and calm.

"I don't know what has happed to the form that was sent to you, *Ryan,*" he said reading his nametag, "but our 171-H was sent to this Embassy three months ago, so I suggest you make us an appointment for right now." Ryan's eyes scanned the form and his voice cracked when he spoke.

"Well, Mr. DiTommaso….as you have the original…it's just that…we had to move our offices in the middle of the night…there were some terrorists…people were shot….some things may have been left behind." He looked down nervously. "You're very lucky you have the original."

"I don't believe in luck, Ryan," Tony said calmly.

"We will process your application right away. Please have a seat," he said nervously moving away from our lion. We sat in the plastic chairs and waited.

Eventually Ryan came and escorted us into the billiard room where we had our "appointment". The room was dark and we actually sat at a pool table with a pool table light illuminating our paperwork on the green felt. We were asked many questions and required to produce even more proof of who we were and why we were there. We were then escorted back to the waiting area. We waited a long time and finally Ryan arrived and handed us a Visa.

"Your son is free to leave the country," he whispered looking cautiously at our lion. "Have a nice day."

I sat on the floor holding Vitaly and leaning on our lion as we waited for the rest of our party to obtain their visas. Tony made his way around the room checking on everyone and speaking encouragement. Eventually, Demetri gathered us all together. It was afternoon now and we knew daylight had certainly arrived although we had no windows where we were.

"Serge is going to get the van as close to the building as possible. Once you see him you are to move as quickly as possible into the van." We all nodded nervously and I held Vitaly close to my chest. Tony took the stroller, diaper bag and my backpack.

"I've got this stuff. You get him and yourself into the van," he said. I agreed and we made our way to the back exit.

Once outside the cold air and the sunlight hit us. The courtyard behind the embassy had turned into a mob scene. It was shoulder to shoulder people. Some were soldiers some were civilians. I could not make out who they were or why they were there, but my eyes scanned for the white van. I made eye contact with a soldier and when he spoke I knew he was American.

"Cover your baby and run," he said pushing me through. I looked back and saw Tony.

"I'm right behind you," he said. Just then our Lion moved in front of me. As he walked the crowd parted. He looked back at me and began to trot. I began to hurry faster and faster until we were running. I could hear Tony behind me as we climbed up into the van. We sat down and I peeled back Vitaly's little hoodie. He woke up just enough to peak at me with his big, blue eyes and went back to sleep. Tony was sitting next to me now and we let out a big sigh. Serge stared straight ahead in silence.

There were people knocking on the windows of the van and the vehicle was rocking from side to side.

'Did you get your Visa?"

"Where are you from?"

"Are you American?" they were shouting.

"Is everyone ok?" Demetri asked as he finally made his way in.

"Yes, we're all fine," we said. Serge was unable to drive very quickly due to all the people, but he shouted out the window and got us out of the crowd eventually. We drove back to the hotel in silence without the usual sound of Serge's pop music station.

Once back at the hotel we all settled into our rooms. We had not seen much of Sam and Kim and the couple from Illinois except that day going to the Embassy because of the warning of Demetri to stay in our rooms.

That evening there was another knock at the door. Tony opened the door to see Brian, the husband from the Illinois couple.

"Look man, we're getting out of here tonight," he whispered. "My wife's really scared and we just don't want to stay here two more days and take any chances. We just wanted to wish you and your family the best. You should call and see about getting an earlier flight," he said. Tony said a few words and I heard the hard pat of a man hug.

"Here's our address. God bless, man," Brian said as he left.

"You too, Brian, be safe. Maybe we can all get together in the states," Tony said as he closed the door. I stood up.

"Are you sure we're ok?" I said. He hugged me.

"God did not bring us this far to leave us now, Suz."

That night we got the video camera out. Vitaly was asleep in the suitcase and we were quite giddy. I assumed the Lion still had my rabbit and I wasn't worried about him. Tony suggested I tell the story of what happened that day so that we can look back and remember someday. I stood in front of the door and began to whisper the details of the day's events.

"You'll have to speak up," he said from behind the camera. I was whispering very loudly now. He started laughing.

"Suzie, there's not a Russian spy behind the door listening to you with a water glass and a tape recorder," he chuckled. I began to giggle too. He was still filming and I tried to convince him not to film me cracking up.

"It's good," he said. "Keep going." It was, despite the impending situation around us, one of the best nights of my life.

Chapter 25

Two days later we packed up our bags and headed for the airport. We were going to arrive a few days before Easter in the United States with our brand new son and I was so ready to go home. We arrived at the Moscow airport and I walked Vitaly back and forth in his stroller. He was starting to make little, tiny noises. He noticed his own reflection in a shop window and I turned the stroller to allow him to see himself. His eyes got very big and he seemed delighted and amazed at himself moving in the reflection. He seemed so small, so small and fragile but the life in him was so strong. We waited a long time to board and we all got quite tired. The flight home was long and Vitaly was very limp. He was so exhausted and had not been eating or drinking much at all. We prayed over him and tried to keep him comfortable.

When we began the descent to JFK airport there was a collective sigh of relief on the plane. There were many couples on that flight who had been through the embassy experience and were glad to be landing on US soil. The customs officers greeted us cheerfully. *I thought New Yorkers were supposed to be rude,* I thought to myself. But compared to what we had been through they were like our party hosts. Our flight to Cleveland wasn't for a couple of hours and we settled into a passenger waiting area with rows and rows of bright blue seats and red carpeting.

"Go call everyone," Tony said. I looked around and located a payphone. I called my parents. My mother sounded so relieved to hear that we were in New York.

"How is he?" she asked.

"He's ok, mum, he's very small and he's been through a lot but he'll be ok," I said reassuringly. There was a long silence.

"Ok, well look. I don't know who will be at the Cleveland airport to meet you. It may just be me and dad," she said.

"What do you mean?" I was shocked and stared at the silver numbers on the keypad of the payphone. What could be so important that our families would miss greeting our new tiny family member? She didn't really answer me but said they had to leave so that they could be in Cleveland to meet us.

"Bring a car seat!" I shouted as she was hanging up.

I walked back to Tony and Vitaly and told Tony what she had said. Sam was playing with Vitaly and Vitaly was giggling.

Sam was making an exaggerated pinching motion with his fingers and saying "Pinchy gonna get you." Vitaly would giggle and squeal. It was the first time I had seen or heard him giggle and all else seemed to fade away. The boarding announcement was made for the Michigan folks. We all looked at each other and sighed, so glad to be on the other side of our journey. We hugged Sam and Kim goodbye and watched as they boarded their flight for Michigan.

Our flight was called and we knew it was only another couple of hours and we would be home. We held hands the whole way. Upon arrival at the Cleveland airport we made our way down the ramp into the receiving area. I saw my Dad waving and my Mum on her tiptoes trying to see. Then I saw my brother in law Mark and sister in law, Rene and one of my best friends, Tia. They were all crying and wearing "It's a Boy!" banners across their chests. They greeted us somewhat carefully.

"Are you all ok?"   I kept hearing.

"Yes, yes, we're just glad to be home." we said. There were lots of hugs and tears but something was not being said. I could sense sadness but dismissed it. After all, they had all been very worried about us.

We carpooled back to our house in my sister-in-law's big SUV after we had figured out the car seat for the first time. We were all piling out of the cars and our neighbors were waiting for us but again something seemed very somber. I thought everyone was just overwhelmed with emotion. We carried Vitaly up to his brand new room and brand new crib. The love I felt for him was overwhelming.

"Welcome home," I whispered as we laid him down. He was asleep. I felt a hand on my shoulder and turned to see Tony's dad in the dark. He hugged us both and looked into the crib. Tears streamed down his cheeks. He looked at Tony.

"Is he ok?" Tony nodded. "You did good, son," he said.

We quietly left Vitaly in his new bed and went back to the kitchen. Everyone was standing, leaning on the counters staring at the floor. *Why was everyone so quiet?* I thought. Just then the back door opened and John, another one of Tony's brothers, walked in. He was crying and his wife Ellen was behind him. She was also crying.

"He's ok guys," I said thinking they were distraught about us. John looked at us.

"Ellen's Mom is dead. We buried her today," he said. The words just hung in the air. I felt my knees giving out. I thought about my phone conversation from Russia with Ellen two days before when I had asked her how much Tylenol to use and I began to cry. We didn't sleep much that night despite our exhaustion.

Chapter 26

We stayed in the barn for a very long time. The storm was beginning to subside and the world seemed a little less hostile.

"You can do this," he said. We were both lying on our sides with our heads together.

"I can try," I said encouragingly.

"I'll be here if you come back, but the truth is you don't need me."

"I do need you…" I knew he was right. "Can I tell you something?"

"Of course," he looked at me warmly.

"I've never been able to talk like this to anyone. My pain has always been so completely unspeakable." I had never thought of that before. "It's just so… unspeakable," I stared at his little gray face, "That's why you're here, isn't it?"

He blinked slowly and smiled. "Go quickly. You've got work to do."

I covered him up with the blanket and kissed his little gray head. "Thank you. I love you."

"Go!" He laughed at my lingering.

"I'm going." I laughed through my tears.

"Bye," he whispered.

"Bye," I said and turned to go. "I love you," I whispered.

He snuggled down under the blanket to show me he was fine, and I quickly went out the man door gently closing it behind me. I started down the long path to the road below. The wind was cold and I felt very alone. I pulled my coat around myself and stopped on the path. I stood motionless. Suddenly I turned and ran back up the path. Panting I tried to silence my breath as I reached the barn door. I gently and quietly opened the door just enough to peek my head around. The blanket was there but he was gone.

The next morning I unpacked our bags, played with Vitaly while Tony went to the store and bought everything he could think of that Vitaly might eat. He also bought a giant NUK bottle nipple and a bottle of Kayro syrup. He cut a big x in the nipple, covered it with sugar syrup and filled with Gatorade. He handed it to me and we prayed as I put it in Vitaly's mouth. To our surprise he grabbed onto that nipple and began to drink like we had never seen. He drank the whole bottle and let out a big burp. What a relief! My Mum came right back that next day and said she had to "get a good look at him." I must have changed his clothes 5 times that day. He started to smile much more and was showing definite signs of recuperation.

Over the next 48 hours he made amazing strides and began to roll over and smile and talk much to the delight of all the friends and family who came to meet him. He was quite a celebrity and seemed to eat it up. The attention and the food, that is. It was a roller coaster of emotion to be so happy and yet so broken hearted for our family's loss. I'm not sure how we got through.

We tried to be there for each other as much as possible. On one hand there was such great loss and grief in our family on the other hand there was such great joy and expansion to our family that it was hard to know what to feel and when.

It was only a few days later that it was Easter Sunday and we had Vitaly in the glass enclosed cry room at church. Pastor John made the happy announcement that my parents had welcomed a brand new grandson in church and we held him up to the glass like a new prince while everyone cheered. It was awesome.

The next few months were a bit of a struggle. Vitaly was great; he was growing by leaps and bounds and was the light of our world. I was so in love with this little boy and could not take my eyes or hands off him. I however, was not used to juggling the baby and the rabbit. I had turned 30 that summer and my rabbit turned 13. It was exhausting. I began to really want to part with my rabbit. He was very heavy and trying to carry him everywhere was really breaking me down. I usually left him at home on the bed. I would spend hours with Vitaly playing and giggling and dressing him and going for walks in our new jogger stroller and then I would come home and there would be my rabbit. I felt attached to him, like I owed it to him to keep him around. I felt like it was my responsibility to continue to have him in my custody and I continued to try to balance them both.

    My experience in Russia had really shown me that I was so much stronger than I had ever imagined and yet I was not strong enough to let go of this security rabbit, or whatever he was. I wasn't even sure myself. Even if I wanted to give him up to whom would I give him? Where would I put him? It was hopeless and I resigned myself to juggle the both of them. I left him on the bed, and I ate just enough to keep us both at a manageable size.

Chapter 27

Driving to Pittsburgh every Sunday with a new baby was trying and we had found a church close to home called Victory and we loved it there. We had been attending Victory for several years, me carrying my rabbit and avoiding the nursery and Tony carrying Vitaly and volunteering for everything under the sun to make up for me. One Sunday in 2003 we decided to go back to Pittsburgh to my parents' church for a visit. We often did that and went to lunch afterward. This particular Sunday there was live testimony. It was a friend of our family named Sarah.

She stood up and walked up to the podium. She began to tell us a story of her abortion as a young woman. She said that word, out loud. I thought I would surely die in my seat. I could hear those sirens again and wanted the earth to swallow me up. Tony squeezed my hand and I tried to hum in my head to drown it out. Despite my efforts not to listen I heard a great deal of what she said. She talked about healing and being made whole again.

Then she began to talk about *her* rabbit in great detail. I had no idea anyone else even had a rabbit. I felt like my rabbit was enormous that day and everyone could see him, especially Sarah. I tried to shove him down in my purse but he was sticking out all over the place. I was just numb after the service. We went to lunch with my Mum and Dad and I had some sort of teriyaki chicken and I made a fuss because I didn't like the peanut sauce, anything to distract myself or anybody else at that table from what we might really be thinking.

It was that night that I really broke down. After I had put Vitaly down to bed I sat on the kitchen floor with my huge rabbit in my lap. I had the church bulletin with Sarah's phone number and tight grip on a glass of wine. I felt weighed down and cluttered with stuff.

I was so nervous when I dialed the number. It rang. Once…twice and then I heard her voice.

"This is Sarah," she said. There was a long pause.

"Me too…the summer of my 17th birthday," I said. There was a long silence.

"Okay" she said very tenderly. Not "It's okay." Just "Okay." *What had I gotten myself into?* I thought. Then slowly we began to talk, to share, to cry. I remember I had drunk the whole glass of wine before I called and at that moment I was wishing I hadn't. My head was spinning. We decided we would talk again.

"Maybe, we could have lunch?" I asked. *Shut up.* I thought. *Why did I say that?*

"Yes, let's make a plan," she said. "I'll have to check my schedule and call you back." I hung up and felt, vulnerable, the same, eager and regretful all together. It was a step, a move in the right direction. Who knows, maybe it was nothing.

Several weeks passed and I came through the door after work.

"Someone called for you, Sarah somebody; she's still on the machine." Tony said from the other room. I felt a sudden sense of panic and relief…it's hard to explain. I pressed the button on the answering machine and waited. She said that she had been terribly ill and was just now beginning to recover but that she wanted to see me. She said that some others had called and they were setting up a meeting.

"We're meeting Monday night at the church," she said. The idea of it scared the daylights out of me. The thought of all of us together in the same room, quietly, looking at each other. *Who would go first? Who would say what they really felt? Would we say that word? Would we say that word over and over until I wanted to scream? Would we look each other in the eye and feel connected somehow? Monday…oh my.*

Monday morning arrived. Tony hugged me and my rabbit before I left.

"I love you. Don't feel that you have to do this. I think you are wonderful," he said. He always knows what to say or, at least up until now. *I am not wonderful*, I thought looking at my rabbit. *Oh my soul, I will go, I have to go.*

    I drove the hour south after work and sat in the parking lot. I saw a couple of vehicles. *Is that one of them?* I thought as I watched a woman enter the building. I said a prayer, grabbed my Bible and rabbit, and walked nervously into a side door. There was a small room ahead and I could hear voices. I know that God was holding me up and pushing me forward because every fiber of my being wanted to turn and run the other direction.

    I entered the room and there were several ladies already there. Sarah introduced us and I didn't hear one name. I sat down and we made some kind of small talk about road construction. It was ridiculous when I think about it, construction. Sarah stood up and closed the door. I felt like I was finally on the verge of something that was so incredibly scary but so incredibly wonderful. As if divinely comforted, it seemed logical. I felt as if someone had said "Not only will I hold your hand and listen to you but, I will commit to hold your hand and listen to you until you don't want me to anymore." I felt my shoulders relax, and I settled into my chair. Sarah began with a prayer. Then she told us that the way it is most often done is to go around the room and just tell your story, however you feel you can, as much or little as you want to share. Sarah went first.

Sarah. She is so elegant, so beautiful, so powerful and so very, very sweet. She told us her rabbit story and the most prominent element was her love for her family and children. She told us of times in her life when she had been violently angry with her husband and kids. How she used to wear red nail polish. She told of reckless, dangerous behavior. How much she loved the Lord. It made me feel so welcome and secure. *I'm not the only one. I'm actually not crazy after all,* I thought. I noticed however, that Sarah's rabbit was white and had a name. I had always wanted my rabbit to be white. It just seemed that he would be more presentable that way, maybe if he were white, I wouldn't have to hide him. Maybe if he were white I could give him a name.

I don't remember telling my story. I awkwardly held up my big rabbit and showed them his zipper. He was very floppy that day and I stumbled all over my words and I fumbled with him. I don't know if I even made sense. I felt unemotional. I felt somewhat detached from myself like I was someone else. I remember feeling like maybe I wasn't going to be able to heal because I couldn't feel. *This was probably a waste of time*. I thought to myself.

Danielle. I remember thinking Danielle did not want to be there. She was so beautiful and yet she looked as if she had been worried and been crying for days maybe years. She was desperately looking for the door or a way out. Her thoughts were scattered. She was terrified. She dropped her rabbit on the floor several times. *She is not ready. The Lord will bring her in His timing,* I thought. She never came back.

    Vanessa. She reminded me of someone I would have known in high school. She was very "together". She rocked and rocked confidently in her chair and listened intently to everyone. My instincts said that she seemed like someone who would always know the right thing to say. I came to learn that this instinct was so very right. She began to tell the story of an alcoholic home, a failed marriage, and the immense love she has for her children and her husband. I remember thinking, *she is a great Mom.* She communicated her desire to help women in crisis pregnancies. *Lucky women,* I thought. She had her rabbit in a special bag which looked like it was custom made, hand embroidered possibly. He was strapped in. She was very organized.

    Barb. Barb brought her rabbits for her second time but she never took them out of her bag. I didn't understand. I thought this was a healing group. *Didn't she heal?* I started to get nervous. *Did I start a journey that would never end? Just listen*, I told myself. Barb had amazing presence. She seemed like the kind of person who would take control in a meeting and be very competent and capable. She played with the arms on her glasses when she talked. Her nails were always impeccable. She told of her mother who forced her to have an abortion and then blamed her and how that led to another one. She spoke of years of denial, of walking around pretending that she was okay. I knew exactly what she meant. I pictured her feeling insecure and crying at night like I did. I wanted to hug her.

Sarah, Vanessa, Barb and I met every Monday night at the church throughout that summer.   We shared our rabbits openly. During our second session I learned to my great surprise that everyone else's rabbit had a zipper too, except Sarah. Her rabbit was pure, spotless, and white as snow. She was beautiful. I wanted my rabbit to look like hers.

The battle was long and painful and we cried and hugged and prayed together that summer. We unzipped our rabbits and shared what was inside. They were all the same. There was no life inside those zippers. When we were nearing the end I almost didn't want to stop. *Maybe I could repeat the group,* I thought to myself. Sarah said we would have a special final session.

Chapter 28

We all arrived at the church on a Saturday afternoon for our very special final session. We brought food and wanted to savor our last few hours as 'The Girls of Summer.' We put the food in the farmhouse which was on the church property and made our way to the sanctuary.

As we entered, soft worship music played. The sanctuary was warm despite the clouds outside but we didn't care about the weather. I stopped and looked around and thought at that moment how very much I loved these women. We sat in the first few pews and cried together. There was no sound but the worship music and our crying. Gently and quietly the back door opened. I knew it was Him before I even turned around and my heart stood still because I suddenly knew why He was there.

"I guess I've got to give you up for good now," I said through tears looking down at my rabbit. My Lion walked slowly towards the altar. He seemed even bigger that day than ever. Most of his body was above the pews, and He gracefully strode up the altar steps. The ground shook as his big paws hit with each step. Once on the altar He turned and stood majestically. He was so graceful and so powerful. He looked at each of us and His perfectly loving eyes looked deep into each of us.

Barb slowly rose from the pew. She was crying and she hugged her rabbits as she approached the altar. She laid them at the feet of the Lion of Judah. They were limp and bruised. Their fur was mangled around their zippers just like mine. We all wept as she laid them at His feet. Sarah nodded to Vanessa. She had unstrapped her rabbit from its custom made bag several weeks earlier and was now holding it every week. I heard the shudder of her cries as she stood up and her body shook. *Be brave,* I thought, *He's my Lion. He's not going to hurt him.* She bravely placed her battered rabbit next to Barb's and collapsed at the altar rail.

I hugged my rabbit tight and considered not taking him up. *I could always come back again right? Like Barb had. I could repeat the process.* I looked at my Lion and took a deep breath. I was standing now and walking toward Him. In that moment I imagined Beth handing her daughter to the social worker that day in the hospital. *I can be brave like she was,* I thought to myself. I kissed my rabbit on his head and placed him at the feet of the lion. My throat had a huge lump in it and I could barely form any words. I looked up at the lion's face. Tears fell like rain.

"Look what I've done," I sobbed. "I'm so sorry." I whispered, slowly backing away from the altar.

We all sat on the floor of the sanctuary with our arms around each other and watched the altar carefully.

The Lion of Judah lifted His massive head to heaven and began to roar. It was a louder, greater roar than I had ever heard Him make. He closed his eyes and tears began to steam down his big cheeks, through his whiskers and onto the altar. His body seemed to become weak and His legs were shaking. He was swaying and vibrating from His own sheer volume. We watched in shocked silence as He continued. It was a howl and a roar. It was sad and it was angry. It shook the windows of the building. We sobbed as we watched Him. He seemed to be suffering and we wanted Him to stop.

Slowly as we watched, the Lion's fur began to turn snowy white. The light began to shine brightly off his snow white fur so much so that every shadow in the room seemed to be chased away. The room was glowing with light and I stared at my rabbit. He was also slowly turning white! He was turning that same pure, snow white. I watched his zipper heal, his bruises were disappearing, he was shrinking and I watched in awe as he turned into a pure white, baby bunny. The roaring continued and we had to cover our eyes and our ears at moments.

Eventually the roaring began to subside and the Lion lay down on the altar next to the pure white bunnies. He was calm and quiet then. He was panting and He nodded to us. I got up and moved toward the altar. He nudged my spotless, white baby toward me. I placed my arms around His big neck and hugged Him.

"Thank you," I whispered into His soft furry ear, my face wet with tears. I wasn't sure if they were my tears or His.   I reached down and scooped up my baby embracing him as I walked down from the altar. His zipper was gone. He was warm and he was without spot or blemish and his ears were pink and so very soft when I stroked them.

"I won't have to hide you anymore," I whispered excitedly. The others went one by one to the lion's feet, retrieved their white bunnies, and sobbed as they kissed our Lion.

We all stood in silence as He got up from the altar. He walked slowly over to Sarah who gave him a knowing nod and hugged His massive neck.

"Thank you," she said as she kissed His cheek. Their encounter was tender as if they had known each other for a long time. He lowered His head and slowly strode down the aisle with His massive tail swishing gently.   Then suddenly I felt my bunny moving his back legs. He wanted to follow. I hugged him again and stared at him.

"I don't want to let you go." I turned to Sarah who had big tears in her eyes. She nodded toward the Lion of Judah.

"I guess I have to let you go now… James." I had never said his name before. I sobbed through my tears. I kissed his white, fluffy head. He was warm and nuzzled me back. I set him down and he hopped toward the Lion. The others followed suit and tearfully said goodbye to their bunnies by name. They all gathered in the aisle behind Him.

The lion looked back as if to lead them but they behaved just like baby bunnies and didn't go in straight line. He had to stop several times to herd them up gently but eventually He led them out the door, and the light in the room returned to normal. I looked down at my arms; they were empty. It was not so much the negative empty, but it was more like unconstrained, free. We all came together with our empty arms and fully embraced each other for the first time, unhindered and wept joyful tears of freedom.

———————————

As I ran, I rounded the bend from Hespenheide Road onto the old path. I opened the gate and closed it again strong and steady. I began to run through the long tunnel of newly green trees. The leaves were fresh and bright. Spring was in full bloom. I made my way to the first clearing and stopped momentarily. I stood looking at the old hay barn. It looked faded and older, the weeds were grown up all around, and l noticed heavy chains and padlocks secured all the doors. Nope, not in the there, I thought to myself.

I began to run again. I felt strong and powerful as I ran up the path to the next tier of the hill. A little brown bunny stood frozen in fear on the side of the path.

"Hi bunny!" I shouted and he darted off into the underbrush.

I continued to run my heart pounding. Up and up I climbed. I came to the end of the wooded path and it spat me out into the giant clearing at the top of Old Orchard Hill. The sun was high and beautiful and not a cloud in the clear blue sky. The fields were fresh, green, and new and dotted with familiar purple, white, and yellow flowers all in clusters. I stood and took a deep breath.

"James!" I shouted as loud as I could and my eyes searched back and forth over the fields.

The meadow was teaming with living creatures. Grasshoppers, crickets, butterflies all moving like waves of life. Suddenly, I saw the grass moving. It created a zig-zag line and it was moving fast. I could just see his little ears as he leapt and bound toward me.

He burst through the long grass and stood on the tractor path.

I gasped. "Look at you!" I said putting both my hands over my mouth. He was pure white without any markings. His ears were pink and covered in fine white fur and his eyes were bright and lively. He stood on his hind legs proudly showing himself off. Then suddenly he dropped down on all fours.

"Look at you," he said with amazement. I looked down and realized I too was dressed in bright white. My arms and legs beaming light without spot or blemish. I bent down and he leapt into my arms. I hugged him tight and felt his soft white fur.

"No zipper?" I didn't even look.

"No zipper," he shook his head.

All around his head the fur was longer like a lion's mane. I stroked it and looked into his eyes.

"I'm a Lionhead," he said beaming with pride.

"Yes you are," I said laughing as tears of happiness fell onto his pure, white fur. He felt light and easy and he was so beautiful. "I understand, James." I said looking deep into his eyes. "I understand it all."

He laughed, "No you don't, but you understand enough...for now."

I smiled and the two of us looked out onto the horizon. The place was so striking that day. Everything was perfect. Then I noticed Him way off in the distance, my Lion. He was huge, majestic and stood boldly seemingly on the edge of the world as He stood separating earth and sky. I stared at Him. I couldn't take my eyes off Him.

Suddenly the green field was parted with a new path. It was a narrow path. I knew it had not been created by a tractor because it was a single lane and it led all through the fields and up to the lion.

"Is that the way?" I whispered.

"That's the only way," he said confidently.

"I will miss you," I said softly

"No you won't," he winked and twitched his nose. I held him gently.

"Will I see you again?" I asked feeling a bit more serious.

"Yes. You will see me again," he replied softening his tone. "I'll be there when it's time for you to come home."

I pulled him in close and savored him. "I love you," I said.

"I love you too." His mouth was close to my ear. "Live free like me," he said quietly.

I set him down and he hopped a few steps positioning himself on the narrow path.

He winked at me. "Special assignments, don't ever forget." Then he turned and began to run. Powerfully he ran. His paws seemed to barely touch the ground as he bound and although he looked smaller and smaller he was more powerful the closer he got to the top of the hill and the Lion. I watched in awe as the two of them slowly disappeared out of sight over the very top of Old Orchard Hill.

Wiping my happy tears, I regained my composure, turned and started back down the path. I was by myself, but I didn't feel alone. I smiled as I walked down the hill, past the abandoned barn and thought about all the life that I had to live and my "special assignments". I started to skip and hop as I ran down the last part of the path to Old Orchard Hill.

When I reached the end of the path I pushed open the gate and stepped out. I closed it behind me and the bar made a loud clank as it connected with the latch. I suddenly heard the sound of chains. I turned back and stared as a large chain and padlock appeared and wove themselves securely around the keyless latch locking it for good.

I smiled, turned around, and stepped boldly and joyfully out into freedom.

THE END.

Do you feel like you carry a burden and you're not sure how to put it down?

Right here, right now say "Lord Jesus, I can't carry this anymore. I'm so very sorry. I trust you and I'm laying it down at your feet and I won't come back for it."

You may have to do it several times in order for <u>you</u> to believe it. But know that He takes it when you lay it at His feet. Now go and be free.

Healing Resources:

www.surrenderingthesecret.com

www.forgivenandsetfree.com

Made in the USA
Charleston, SC
19 March 2013